Praying Your Way to a Fearless Life

Carey Scott

Praying Your Way
to a
Fearless
Life

200
Inspiring Prayers
for a
Woman's Heart

BARBOUR
PUBLISHING

Print ISBN 978-1-63609-010-8

Published by Barbour Publishing, Inc., 1810 Barbour Drive, Uhrichsville, Ohio 44683, www.barbourbooks.com

Our mission is to inspire the world with the life-changing message of the Bible.

Member of the
Evangelical Christian
Publishers Association

Printed in China.

Fearless in the Battles

Dear God, I know You command me to be strong and courageous, but sometimes I don't feel that way. Instead, I feel weak. I hide away in fear of how things might turn out. I start to believe lies about my future. And I cower at the thought of standing strong. I need You to give me strength and bravery so I can be obedient to Your call on my life. I need constant reminders that You are with me at all times. I need to know that You will direct my path every step of the way. I'm choosing to believe that You will help me be fearless in the face of every battle that comes my way. In Jesus' name I pray, amen.

*This is My command: be strong and courageous.
Never be afraid or discouraged because I am
your God, the Eternal One, and I will
remain with you wherever you go.*
Joshua 1:9 voice

TRUTH OVER INTIMIDATION

Dear God, I am intimidated by so many people. It seems like everyone makes me feel inferior because I see them as better than me. I believe they matter more. Why do I always think that way? I know that You made me on purpose, so why don't I see my worth? I'm afraid I'll always feel less than others because of the way I look, the way I act, or a million other things. Give me the courage to believe I am who You say I am. Help me stand strong in the truth that I'm made on purpose and for a purpose. Make me brave enough to believe I have value and worth because of who I am on the inside. In Jesus' name I pray, amen.

"Be strong. Take courage. Don't be intimidated. Don't give them a second thought because GOD, your God, is striding ahead of you. He's right there with you. He won't let you down; he won't leave you."

DEUTERONOMY 31:6 MSG

THE CONSTANT BATTLE OF FEAR AND WORRY

Dear God, I know Your Word says I wasn't created to be a coward, but there are times I second-guess that. It seems I'm constantly battling fear and worry. I'm afraid of making mistakes and embarrassing myself. I'm scared of saying the wrong thing when it matters the most. I worry about forgetting important things or missing a milestone in the life of someone I love. I'm terrified of doing the one thing that will end a relationship that means so much to me. I know in my head fear isn't from You. Please make that truth reign in my heart! Help me stand, knowing I have baked right into me a well-balanced mind, discipline, and self-control. In Jesus' name I pray, amen.

For God did not give us a spirit of timidity
(of cowardice, of craven and cringing and
fawning fear), but [He has given us a spirit]
of power and of love and of calm and
well-balanced mind and discipline and self-control.

2 TIMOTHY 1:7 AMPC

STRENGTH IN CONVICTIONS

Dear God, it's hard to hold on to my convictions in today's world. It feels like society is working overtime to demoralize me for my values, making me feel irrelevant. They preach blatant immorality, and when anyone stands up against it, that person is blasted. I'm fearful to speak up. Inside I may hold my convictions tight, but I'm afraid to speak them out loud. I don't want to live my one and only life shut down like that. And I know it's not how You intended me to live either. I want my life to point others to You in heaven. Let my words and actions make a strong case for being a Christ follower. In Jesus' name I pray, amen.

Keep your eyes open, hold tight to your convictions, give it all you've got, be resolute, and love without stopping.
1 CORINTHIANS 16:13–14 MSG

The Courage to Be You

Dear God, I'm in a season of wanting to give up. I'm done trying to be who everyone wants me to be. I feel like I'm not good enough for some people, either too much or too little. It's exhausting. I worry what their response might be if I decided to just be me instead of getting caught up in trying to please them. I want to be liked. I want to fit in. I want to be loved. Your Word tells me to be brave, and so I am asking for help so I can be. I need to have hope that I'll be accepted. For now I'll keep believing in Your promise of courage delivered. In Jesus' name I pray, amen.

Here's what I've learned through it all:
Don't give up; don't be impatient; be entwined
as one with the Lord. Be brave and courageous,
and never lose hope. Yes, keep on waiting—
for he will never disappoint you!
PSALM 27:14 TPT

THE CONFIDENCE
TO BE HONEST

Dear God, help me find the confidence to be honest with others. Strengthen me with Your strength. Embolden me with Your power. Whether it's sharing my opinion about a situation, giving advice when asked, offering my ideas in a meeting, or just being truthful with a loved one, give me the courage to be candid. I can't do this without You. Bless me with the wisdom to know when to be authentic in loving and kind ways, and let me know when I should be bold and frank. Please give me the discernment to know the difference. I trust You to empower me with the self-assurance I need to navigate these situations every time. In Jesus' name I pray, amen.

The wicked are edgy with guilt, ready to run off even when no one's after them; honest people are relaxed and confident, bold as lions.

PROVERBS 28:1 MSG

WHEN YOU'RE SCARED
TO TRUST GOD

Dear God, can I be honest? I'm terrified to trust You. It's not that You've ever let me down—You haven't. It's not that I don't believe in You—I do. But it's so hard for me to let go of control and hand my life over to someone I cannot see with my eyes and touch with my hand. Sometimes it feels like I'm trusting air, and it scares me. Grow my faith. Help me realize Your ways are far superior to mine. And help me remember Your heart for me is always good. From today forward, I want to surrender control and learn to follow Your leading. Help me set aside fear and choose to trust You. In Jesus' name I pray, amen.

*Trust in the Lord completely, and do not
rely on your own opinions. With all your heart
rely on him to guide you, and he will lead you
in every decision you make. Become intimate
with him in whatever you do, and he
will lead you wherever you go.*

PROVERBS 3:5–6 TPT

THE STRENGTH TO KEEP WORKING

Dear God, today's verse offers me a great reminder to trust that You'll help me finish the work I've been called to do. Thank You—because I need it! The truth is I usually start out strong in projects and tasks, but my courage often wanes when I come up against problems or criticism. They discourage me and derail my focus. And I find myself scared that I'll mess up or let people down, which effectively keeps me from moving forward. I don't want to live in fear. Instead, I want my faith to be solid, believing You won't leave me to figure everything out on my own. I need You, Father. Without Your help, I'm unable to be strong and courageous. In Jesus' name I pray, amen.

Also David told Solomon his son, Be strong and courageous, and do it. Fear not, be not dismayed, for the Lord God, my God, is with you. He will not fail or forsake you until you have finished all the work for the service of the house of the Lord.

1 CHRONICLES 28:20 AMPC

Remaining Undaunted

Dear God, how am I supposed to be undaunted when my life is full of stress and strife? I look at the state of the world, and it terrifies me. Everyone is bickering, and our nation is divided. I'm struggling in some very important relationships, and it worries me. I'm scared about my financial obligations and lack of income. I'm concerned with my health but too afraid to go talk to a doctor. I'm not sure I could handle a bad diagnosis. My work isn't fulfilling, and I feel hopeless about it. Lord, I need the kind of peace and confidence that comes from You. I am desperate for the fear to take a backseat to my faith. In Jesus' name I pray, amen.

I have told you these things, so that in Me you may have [perfect] peace and confidence. In the world you have tribulation and trials and distress and frustration; but be of good cheer [take courage; be confident, certain, undaunted]! For I have overcome the world. [I have deprived it of power to harm you and have conquered it for you.]
John 16:33 AMPC

THE CONFIDENCE
TO EXPECT GOD

Dear God, Your Word says that I should expect You to show up in my life. So why do I live in constant fear that You won't be there when I need You? I worry I've sinned too much or angered You one too many times. I feel certain my choices disappoint You on the regular. Sometimes I convince myself that You have bigger issues to deal with and that my asking is nothing more than an inconvenience. I need a shift in perspective so I can live in expectation of You! I want to know without a doubt that Your hands are deep in the frustrations I'm experiencing. And I need God-given confidence that You'll show up. In Jesus' name I pray, amen.

Be brave. Be strong. Don't give up.
Expect God to get here soon.
PSALM 31:24 MSG

BRAVE ENOUGH TO BELIEVE

Dear God, I can't do this without You. My heart is heavy, and I'm burdened with the weight of life right now. I don't see a way out of the mess I am in, and it freaks me out. It makes me wonder why I even try. I know You say everything is possible with Your help, but sometimes that feels like a pie-in-the-sky wish. In the ups and downs of life, it's hard to trust anyone but myself. But having faith means I choose to trust Your words over my feelings. It means I ask You for the things I need, believing they will be given to me when I need them. Help me live brave like that. In Jesus' name I pray, amen.

I know what it means to lack, and I know what it means to experience overwhelming abundance. For I'm trained in the secret of overcoming all things, whether in fullness or in hunger. And I find that the strength of Christ's explosive power infuses me to conquer every difficulty.

PHILIPPIANS 4:12–13 TPT

The Fear of Rejection

Dear God, it's discouraging to hear what others are saying about me. It's like my greatest fears of rejection and judgment are coming true. I actually thought I was liked. I thought I had good friends who loved and cared for me. But it seems I thought I was more liked than I really am. Would You please help me remember I was created on purpose and with a purpose? Whisper into my spirit what makes me lovable in Your eyes. Show me what makes me unique and special. Grow my confidence in who I am because of You and not anything else. And keep me from anchoring my sense of worth in anything the world has to offer. In Jesus' name I pray, amen.

Jesus overheard what they were talking about and said to the leader, "Don't listen to them; just trust me."

Mark 5:36 MSG

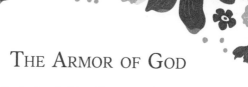

THE ARMOR OF GOD

Dear God, thank You for providing heavenly armor that I can access whenever I need it. I'm grateful You created a way to keep me safe and give me confidence. I'm also thankful this armor offers powerful protection against anything that comes my way, be it a scheme in the spirit or a battle here on earth. This armor delivers courage that I will be able to face my fears knowing I'm backed by You. It encourages bravery as I take steps forward in my journey to live a full life. And it reminds me of how much You must love me to make sure I am not left unprotected and unarmed. In Jesus' name I pray, amen.

Put on the full armor of God to protect
yourselves from the devil and his evil schemes.
We're not waging war against enemies of flesh
and blood alone. No, this fight is against tyrants,
against authorities, against supernatural powers
and demon princes that slither in the darkness of
this world, and against wicked spiritual armies
that lurk about in heavenly places.
EPHESIANS 6:11–12 VOICE

THE SECURITY THAT LEADS TO COURAGE

Dear God, yesterday I learned that You provided armor to protect me in battles. Your armor is meant to give me victory over fear that keeps me captive and unable to experience all that You have planned for my life. Today I am choosing to secure the belt of truth around my waist to strengthen me against any lies. I'm choosing to wear the breastplate of holiness that protects my heart from wrong influences. And I'm standing ready to share Your goodness with those around me. What an honor to wear armor that glorifies You and blesses me. Thank You for knowing I would need this kind of security to muster the courage to face my hardest and scariest days. In Jesus' name I pray, amen.

Put on truth as a belt to strengthen you to stand in triumph. Put on holiness as the protective armor that covers your heart. Stand on your feet alert, then you'll always be ready to share the blessings of peace.

EPHESIANS 6:14–15 TPT

WEAPONS FOR VICTORY

Dear God, thank You for knowing that the weapons I need to navigate the ups and downs of this life are not earthly ones. Because my battles are waged in the heavenlies, my arsenal needs to be filled with spiritual armaments. Help me remember my shield of faith is available every time hard seasons hit and fear sets in. I know it will steady me to press into You for wisdom and peace. As I choose to trust Your faithfulness, that invaluable piece of armor will help stop the burning arrows of hate fired right at me. And Your Word, the sword of the Spirit, will teach and instruct me how to live a courageous life of victory rather than defeat. In Jesus' name I pray, amen.

Don't forget to raise the shield of faith above all else, so you will be able to extinguish flaming spears hurled at you from the wicked one. Take also the helmet of salvation and the sword of the Spirit, which is the word of God.
EPHESIANS 6:16–17 VOICE

EMPOWERED PRAYER

Dear God, Your Word says to pray at all times and with all kinds of prayers. It doesn't mince words when it also says to ask for everything I need. This seems like an expectation rather than a suggestion. And honestly, it feels like You're inviting me to talk to You all day long about anything and everything. Whether I am worried or afraid, You want to hear from me. When I feel hopeless, I should pray. When I need Your comfort or guidance, I can talk to You about it. My days would be better if I lived this verse because the enemy wouldn't have any space to stir me up and whisper terrifying thoughts into my heart. Thank You! In Jesus' name I pray, amen.

Pray at all times (on every occasion, in every season) in the Spirit, with all [manner of] prayer and entreaty. To that end keep alert and watch with strong purpose and perseverance, interceding in behalf of all the saints (God's consecrated people).

EPHESIANS 6:18 AMPC

NAVIGATING THE
FEAR OF MARRIAGE

Dear God, I'm worried about my marriage. We've been so busy with kids and work, and it feels like we are two ships passing in the night. Sometimes the distance scares me because we're not as connected as normal. Help us be aware so we can be engaged with each other. Give us hearts full of love and joy, and remind us to carve out time each day to affirm and appreciate the other. And if we are heading into a rough season of marriage, grow my faith to trust You as we navigate the choppy waters with hope. Let me be expectant for good things. And help my heart be secure in You so it's not full of unnecessary fear. In Jesus' name I pray, amen.

They will not live in fear or dread of what
may come, for their hearts are firm,
ever secure in their faith.

PSALM 112:7 TPT

There Is Nothing to Fear

Dear God, I appreciate how boldly Your Word tells me there is nothing to fear. Most of the time, though, I struggle to believe it. I find myself fixating on all that's going wrong. I stare at tough situations that feel hard and hopeless. I stand dismayed at how quickly my circumstances change. And these things breed fear. They make me predict horrible outcomes. They leave my spirit unsettled. I need to look to You for peace. I need to grab hold of Your promise to strengthen me. I need Your help, Lord. Please comfort me with Your presence and share Your perspective so I can find the rest I need for my heart and mind. In Jesus' name I pray, amen.

Fear not [there is nothing to fear], for I am with you; do not look around you in terror and be dismayed, for I am your God. I will strengthen and harden you to difficulties, yes, I will help you; yes, I will hold you up and retain you with My [victorious] right hand of rightness and justice.

Isaiah 41:10 ampc

Victory against Fear and Shame

Dear God, I struggle with guilt and shame. I have messed up so much, making bad choices more than I care to share. Not only does it feel like what I've done is wrong, it feels like who I am is wrong. And it's because of those painful feelings that I've hidden from You. But Your Word says that if I ask, You will give me the ability to stand up to the temptation and make the right choice. What's more, You say every test I face is an opportunity to grow my faith in You as I choose to trust Your helping hand. I don't have to be afraid anymore! I can stand in victory because You've made a way. In Jesus' name I pray, amen.

We all experience times of testing, which is normal for every human being. But God will be faithful to you. He will screen and filter the severity, nature, and timing of every test or trial you face so that you can bear it. And each test is an opportunity to trust him more, for along with every trial God has provided for you a way of escape that will bring you out of it victoriously.

1 Corinthians 10:13 tpt

THE REMEDY FOR PARALYZING FEAR

Dear God, I'm so stressed out trying to predict what others might be plotting against me. I'm paranoid they can't be trusted because I've been in these kinds of situations before that ended badly. In my fear, I freeze up. I lose all bravery and courage to be myself and go about my day. My confidence is shot, and I struggle to stay focused on the good things happening in my life. I'm asking You for steadfast faith, trusting You're not only aware of every detail but also actively working things out. Let me be unshakable. Let faith be my default button. Take every fear away from me so I can live free and with Your peace. In Jesus' name I pray, amen.

Don't be paralyzed in any way by what your opponents are doing. Your steadfast faith in the face of opposition is a sign that they are doomed and that you have been graced with God's salvation.

PHILIPPIANS 1:28 VOICE

THE DESIRE TO BE OPTIMISTIC

Dear God, Your Word clearly says not to be dismayed. It instructs us not to be discouraged or downcast in the battles we face every day. But that's a tall order. How am I supposed to be optimistic when I'm watching important relationships crumble? How can I be hopeful when the doctors aren't optimistic in the treatment plan? How can I be expectant when I look at the state of the world? And Lord, how can I be positive when my finances are failing? I am desperate for peace and joy. I'm tired of feeling negative. I want hope and happiness instead of dismay. Please let these reign in my heart as I place my faith in Your hands. In Jesus' name I pray, amen.

*Then you will prosper if you are
careful to keep and fulfill the statutes
and ordinances with which the Lord
charged Moses concerning Israel.
Be strong and of good courage. Dread
not and fear not; be not dismayed.*
1 Chronicles 22:13 AMPC

Hope for Nighttime Fears

Dear God, nighttime is hard for me. It's when all my fears awaken and keep me preoccupied with terrible endings to the relationships and situations that worry me. I love how Your Word encourages me to seek Your ways and will because it will affect my sleep positively. If I choose to walk with You during the day, the nighttime will reflect that decision. Give me the confidence to stick with You. Help me remember the relationship between Your wisdom and my peace. Let me remember that to keep fear at bay, I must be intentional about spending time in the Word and in prayer. Thank You for making a way to freedom from stress and strife. In Jesus' name I pray, amen.

The wise counsel GOD gives when I'm
awake is confirmed by my sleeping heart.
Day and night I'll stick with GOD; I've got
a good thing going and I'm not letting go.
PSALM 16:7–8 MSG

WHY YOU CAN BE UNAFRAID

Dear God, help me remember that You are the One who saves me. It's not food or alcohol. It's not people or a full calendar. It's not a trendy spiritual awakening or meditation. It's not medication or a new wardrobe. Nothing in the world can save me from my fears and insecurities like You can. Everything else offers short-term relief to a long-term battle. It's because of You, because my trust is firmly planted in Your love, that I can live unafraid. I can be confident in scary times, knowing You promise to be with me always. I can hope because You won't leave me trapped and alone. I receive Your love! In Jesus' name I pray, amen.

"Behold—God is my salvation! I am confident,
unafraid, and I will trust in you." Yes!
The Lord Yah is my might and my melody;
he has become my salvation!
ISAIAH 12:2 TPT

THE WORLD'S PEACE IS FRAGILE

Dear God, I could use a big dose of peace in my life. These days, peace feels terribly elusive. With my crazy life, I am stirred up most of the time. My emotions swirl around me as I try to calm my anxious heart. How do I stop my mind from spinning? How do I find rest when I can't slow my thoughts down? You offer Your peace to those who ask, knowing it will bring a confident stillness that will lead to courage. Too often I look to the world for a remedy, but it only offers a fragile kind of peace that breaks with too much expectation. Lord, please bring Your peace into my life. In Jesus' name I pray, amen.

*"I leave the gift of peace with you—my peace.
Not the kind of fragile peace given by the world,
but my perfect peace. Don't yield to fear or be
troubled in your hearts—instead, be courageous!"*

JOHN 14:27 TPT

With God by Your Side

Dear God, Your Word says that with You by my side I can be free of fear, unafraid of anything that comes my way. It says to lay all my fears out before You and stand in unmovable trust because You will give me the help I need to overcome them. I want to believe it's as simple as that, but I know what's often easy to say is difficult to walk out. Please give me the strength to make decisions that set me up for freedom. Grow my faith so I trust in You with all my heart. I don't want anything to keep me from the peace You promise. And I want to experience it every single day. In Jesus' name I pray, amen.

But in the day that I'm afraid, I lay all my fears before you and trust in you with all my heart. What harm could a man bring to me? With God on my side, I will not be afraid of what comes. The roaring praises of God fill my heart as I trust his promises.

Psalm 56:3–4 TPT

Trusting How God Answers

Dear God, I need the kind of faith that doesn't waver based on Your responses to my prayers. I need to be steadfast in my faith, unshakable in my reliance on You. In my heart, I know You're capable of saving me from my fears and insecurities. I completely believe there is nothing You cannot accomplish. And I trust You will do what is best for me as well as what glorifies Your holy name. You are a good Father! But if You choose to answer my prayers differently than I'd hoped, let me remember You are still worthy of my devotion. You are still a faithful God. And I can still ask You for what I need. In Jesus' name I pray, amen.

If you throw us into the blazing furnace, then the God we serve is able to rescue us from a furnace of blazing fire and release us from your power, Your Majesty. But even if He does not, O king, you can be sure that we still will not serve your gods and we will not worship the golden statue you erected.

Daniel 3:17–18 voice

Brave No Matter What

Dear God, would You please strengthen me! I don't want to be the kind of woman who lives in defeat, afraid of anything and everything that comes my way. Instead, I want to thrive in the victory that only comes from nurturing a trusting faith in You, confident I will receive all I need to stand strong and face the inevitable and difficult storms of life. Help me find courage as I choose You over anything the world offers. My heart's desire is to be fearless, knowing I can do all things through Christ, who gives me strength. I don't want to trust small. I want to believe big! Help me be brave no matter what. In Jesus' name I pray, amen.

*If you faint in the day of adversity,
your strength is small.*
Proverbs 24:10 AMPC

REINFORCED RESOLVE

Dear God, help me remember that ultimately, You're my Defender. I know there are times You require me to advocate for myself and stand up to my fears, but there are other times when You're the One to conquer what opposes me. Either way, I'm so thankful knowing You promise to be with me. I'll be honest, though—sometimes it feels too overwhelming to face my fears even though I know You are present. I worry about what others might think if I stand my ground. So God, in those times, let me feel Your fatherly protection boosting my bravery. Reinforce my resolve. And give me grit and guts to be strong knowing You have my back. In Jesus' name I pray, amen.

Yahweh is my revelation-light and the source of my salvation. I fear no one! I'll never turn back and run, for you, Yahweh, surround and protect me. When evil ones come to destroy me, they will be the ones who turn back.

PSALM 27:1–2 TPT

Surrendering Worries

Dear God, I'm feeling hopeless. I'm worried certain things in my life won't change, and it scares me. Your Word says Jesus came for freedom, but I feel stuck. It says You will fill me to overflowing with joy and peace that cannot be contained, but I am disheartened instead. I'm desperate for You to fill my heart with encouragement that everything will be okay. Would You graciously change my attitude so I can expect Your good works? Let the Holy Spirit replace my overwhelming fears with overwhelming faith. And I would deeply appreciate a shift in perspective so I can surrender my worries as I wait for You to fill me with hopefulness and inspiration for the future! In Jesus' name I pray, amen.

Now may God, the fountain of hope,
fill you to overflowing with uncontainable
joy and perfect peace as you trust in him.
And may the power of the Holy Spirit
continually surround your life with his
super-abundance until you radiate with hope!
ROMANS 15:13 TPT

THE FEAR OF STEPPING OFF THE BOAT

Dear God, I have some big decisions ahead, and they're kind of freaking me out. What a relief to realize You already know every detail. Thank You for seeing the complexity of each choice. The truth is these decisions are requiring me to step way out of my comfort zone, and it's unnerving. It's a mix of excitement and fear. I feel You're calling me out of the boat like Peter, asking me to trust. Help me keep my eyes on You rather than the worrisome circumstances around me. Give me confidence to follow Your lead. I truly believe if I hold on to You through the process, You'll show me the way. Grow my faith so I can follow You each day! In Jesus' name I pray, amen.

He said, "Come ahead." Jumping out of the boat, Peter walked on the water to Jesus. But when he looked down at the waves churning beneath his feet, he lost his nerve and started to sink. He cried, "Master, save me!"
MATTHEW 14:29–30 MSG

FEAR OF FAILING AS A PARENT

Dear God, help me be the best parent I can be. It's the hardest and scariest thing I've ever done. What if I mess up my kids and they turn out to be mean people? What if I don't teach them all they need to know? I feel judged by others. I feel like I am failing woefully. And I feel completely ill-equipped to do this job. You say in Your Word that because You are for me, no one can stand against me. You say You love me and won't withhold help. I need You right now! Please bless me with peace and wisdom. Strengthen me. And remind me I was chosen on purpose to be their mom. In Jesus' name I pray, amen.

So, what does all this mean? If God has determined to stand with us, tell me, who then could ever stand against us? For God has proved his love by giving us his greatest treasure, the gift of his Son. And since God freely offered him up as the sacrifice for us all, he certainly won't withhold from us anything else he has to give.

ROMANS 8:31–32 TPT

THE WEIGHT OF GUILT

Dear God, I feel a million fingers pointing at me all the time. Every day I wake up with a sense of guilt and I can't pinpoint it. I worry that I'm doing something wrong, always expecting to hear a judgmental comment. Why is guilt so oppressive in my life? I know Jesus came to the world and died to remove my sin—and that includes any guilt from my sin. But I cannot seem to shake the guilt. In Your kindness, would You supernaturally lift this from me? If there's something I need to change, I'm listening. But if not, hear my plea to remove this unnecessary guilt. It's too heavy for my heart to carry another day. In Jesus' name I pray, amen.

Who will bring a charge against God's elect people? It is God who acquits them. Who is going to convict them? It is Christ Jesus who died, even more, who was raised, and who also is at God's right side. It is Christ Jesus who also pleads our case for us.

ROMANS 8:33–34 CEB

The Fear of Separation

Dear God, sometimes I'm afraid that my past choices or current season of sinning will cause You to walk away from me in frustration. I worry there is something in my life that will inevitably separate us. I know Your Word is clear when it says there's nothing and no one that can cause that to happen. But honestly, I struggle to believe it because I've done some horrible things—things I've not told anyone. I don't want to waste my life living in the fear that I may cause You to walk away. So would You speak deep into my heart the truth that You will never leave me? Would You settle that in my heart? In Jesus' name I pray, amen.

Who shall ever separate us from Christ's love?
Shall suffering and affliction and tribulation?
Or calamity and distress? Or persecution or
hunger or destitution or peril or sword?
ROMANS 8:35 AMPC

Performance-Based Work Woes

Dear God, I'm ashamed of my job performance. I'm missing deadlines and letting the team down. It's worrisome. I know I'm disappointing my co-workers and those in authority over me, but I'm also concerned about disappointing You. I've been afraid it might cause You to turn away from me. What a relief to read today's verses that say there's not one thing that can cause a break in Your love for me. I'm grateful it isn't performance based. Lord, please help me focus on my work as I rest in knowing it isn't a gauge of my goodness in Your eyes. Help me also to sharpen my skills and be a team player, so I'm an employee with integrity. In Jesus' name I pray, amen.

*For I have every confidence that nothing—
not death, life, heavenly messengers, dark
spirits, the present, the future, spiritual
powers, height, depth, nor any created thing—
can come between us and the love of God
revealed in the Anointed, Jesus our Lord.*
ROMANS 8:38–39 VOICE

A Continual Conversation

Dear God, thank You for reminding me that asking for Your help isn't a once-and-done proposition. Instead, it's an ongoing conversation. It's a continual request. And when I purpose to connect with You daily to grow our personal relationship, it keeps me connected with my source for everything. When I need courage to face my fears, You give it. When I need strength to try again, I get it directly from You. When I need peace and comfort, You provide it. When I'm lacking wisdom or discernment, You are the One who brings it, in spades. Every day, give me confidence to pursue our relationship that I may receive the gifts that come from choosing to walk with You. In Jesus' name I pray, amen.

Pursue the Lord and his strength;
seek his face always!
1 Chronicles 16:11 ceb

Stepping Out of Fear to Lead

Dear God, help me be a leader for those around me. I get nervous at the thought of standing up and speaking out because I don't want to be judged. But I am feeling the call to step out of my comfort zone and lead. Help me find through You the courage to take this next step, the confidence to share my vision, and the bravery to risk negative responses. The goal isn't to please the world; it's to please You. And I know that when You call me to a task, it means You will also give me the skill to walk it out. Remind me too that the goal isn't perfection; it's being purposeful. In Jesus' name I pray, amen.

So stand up! Helping us follow the law is now your responsibility. Do not be afraid; we will support your actions.

Ezra 10:4 voice

THE COURAGE
FOR COMMUNITY

Dear God, I crave to be in community with people. I want friends to spend time with and to walk through life together. But I'm terrified to put myself out there again because it's not gone well in the past. I've been betrayed and left out, judged and criticized, and it's kept me isolated. What if the same thing happens again? Help me find grace to release those who've hurt me and courage to try one more time. You didn't create us to be alone. Your intention has always been for us to be united in one spirit and mind. And Your hope is for me to find a community of people and thrive! Please help me. In Jesus' name I pray, amen.

*Most important, live together in a manner
worthy of Christ's gospel. Do this, whether I
come and see you or I'm absent and hear about
you. Do this so that you stand firm, united in
one spirit and mind as you struggle together
to remain faithful to the gospel.*
PHILIPPIANS 1:27 CEB

A DIVINE BOOST
IN CONFIDENCE

Dear God, would You give me the courage to be an advocating voice in my community? I want to make a difference, but it scares me to be bold. I worry what others might think. I'm nervous that I'll say the wrong thing. I'm anxious others won't care what I have to say. It's just nerve racking. But Lord, I feel You calling me out of my comfort zone into new territory, and I'll need a divine boost in confidence. I care about my community and am passionate to help where I can. Thank You for putting this desire in my heart. Now I'm trusting You to open the right doors and to make me brave to do Your work! In Jesus' name I pray, amen.

Be strong, and let us fight bravely
for the sake of our people and the
cities of our True God, and may the
Eternal do what seems good in His sight.
2 SAMUEL 10:12 VOICE

Producing a Fearlessness

Dear God, I know the last thing I need to do when I'm afraid is run and hide. Even when everything in me wants to pull the covers over my head and disappear, Your encouragement is always to trust in Your will and ways. Your Word says You use all things for my good. You use troubled times to grow my faith, increase my endurance, refine my character, and instill hope. If I try to avoid any rough seasons, I risk missing out on the gifts that come from them. I must choose faith over fear, and I will need Your help. Produce a fearlessness in me that's made possible through trusting You in every situation. In Jesus' name I pray, amen.

But that's not all! Even in times of trouble we have a joyful confidence, knowing that our pressures will develop in us patient endurance. And patient endurance will refine our character, and proven character leads us back to hope. And this hope is not a disappointing fantasy, because we can now experience the endless love of God cascading into our hearts through the Holy Spirit who lives in us!
ROMANS 5:3–5 TPT

HELPLESS AND WEAK
NO LONGER

Dear God, sometimes it's hard to grasp all the ways Jesus' death on the cross saved me. Not only did it make a way back to You and secure eternal life in Your presence, but it also pulled me from helplessness. It made me strong rather than weak. And it has given me the courage I need to navigate some very difficult spaces in life. Your Son's selfless act of love changed me forever, and I am so grateful. Help me find that confidence every time I'm faced with fear. I don't want to be someone who cowers when adversity comes my way. Instead, I want to stand strong, empowered by Jesus' love demonstrated at Calvary. In Jesus' name I pray, amen.

For when the time was right, the Anointed
One came and died to demonstrate his love
for sinners who were entirely helpless, weak,
and powerless to save themselves.

ROMANS 5:6 TPT

WHAT DEFLATES COURAGE

Dear God, Your Word says I should not give up or quit doing the things You've called me to do. It's clear that when I persevere, You bless my stamina and tenacity. I want to be the kind of woman who endures, working with my might until the very end. But sometimes I let fear of failure creep in. I remember all the times I tried and bombed. I recall every bad decision that ended in disaster. When I look at tasks ahead through that lens, it deflates my courage and confidence. Help me remember that perfection isn't the goal. I don't have to be flawless. Remind me that it's my steadfast heart to do good that matters most. In Jesus' name I pray, amen.

So let's not allow ourselves to get fatigued doing good. At the right time we will harvest a good crop if we don't give up, or quit. Right now, therefore, every time we get the chance, let us work for the benefit of all, starting with the people closest to us in the community of faith.

GALATIANS 6:9–10 MSG

Strength from His Presence

Dear God, I think I'm beginning to understand that being strong and having courage is possible when I know You are with me. For so long, I've tried to gut it out myself, relying on my own strength to make myself brave. I've tried to talk myself into having courage. I've tried all the tricks of the trade, like self-care, meditation, visualization, and repeating empowering phrases. In the end, they've all left me fearful and struggling with the same insecurities. But if I take a moment to remember that Your promise is to never leave me alone, I can find confidence and courage from that powerful truth. Thank You for knowing I need You by my side. In Jesus' name I pray, amen.

Then GOD commanded Joshua son of Nun saying, "Be strong. Take courage. You will lead the People of Israel into the land I promised to give them. And I'll be right there with you."
DEUTERONOMY 31:23 MSG

Being Confident in Plans

Dear God, today's verse is so encouraging because it empowers me to speak up and present a positive perspective. There are so many times I feel confident in moving forward but am afraid to voice it to others, especially when groupthink isn't the same as mine. Give me boldness to make a case for what I believe. Let me remember that it's okay when not everyone agrees. And help me not be discouraged by those who don't feel as confident in my plans as I do. There is grace for everyone's opinion! But I trust that if my plans are Your plans, You'll give me the favor I need to bravely take them one more step in the right direction. In Jesus' name I pray, amen.

But Caleb calmed the congregation,
and he spoke to Moses. ["]We should
go straight in, right away, and take
it over. We are surely able![”]
Numbers 13:30 voice

THE EVAPORATION OF FEAR

Dear God, You are very clear in Your Word that fear cannot thrive where Your love resides. There is something so powerful about it—powerful enough to drive every kind of fear away. Specifically, today's verse talks about the fear of punishment. I'll admit I worry about retribution. I stress out about the critical spirit in others. I've been on the receiving end of chastisement one too many times, and it's a terrible experience. It leaves me feeling worthless and unlovable. In those moments, speak loudly into my spirit and remind me that I am loved by You. Because, Lord, I'm choosing to believe that doing so will make the fear evaporate into thin air. In Jesus' name I pray, amen.

Love never brings fear, for fear is always related to punishment. But love's perfection drives the fear of punishment far from our hearts. Whoever walks constantly afraid of punishment has not reached love's perfection.

1 JOHN 4:18 TPT

UNSHAKABLE CONFIDENCE

Dear God, the one thing that stands between me and unshakable confidence is fear. It knocks me to my knees. It undermines my gumption to try again. It talks me out of trusting that You'll help me accomplish meaningful things in my life. I'm tired of being held captive by worry and insecurity. This isn't how life should be. It's not Your best for me. And even though I have faith in You, sometimes it's not enough. From today forward, I'm going to focus on You over my fear. Every time I feel it creeping in, I'm going to pray for Your unshakable confidence to override the worry. Let that act of faith help me become secure in Your love. In Jesus' name I pray, amen.

So now, beloved ones, stand firm, stable, and enduring. Live your lives with an unshakable confidence. We know that we prosper and excel in every season by serving the Lord, because we are assured that our union with the Lord makes our labor productive with fruit that endures.

1 CORINTHIANS 15:58 TPT

A SLIVER OF FAITH

Dear God, I know the way to overcome fear is to anchor my faith in You. I know Your Word says that even a sliver of faith can do mighty things in me and through me. The problem is I worry that the little bit I have is not enough. When my relationships turn rocky, I cower in concern. When my finances or health start to spiral, I'm sidelined by the stress. I rarely stand tall when I'm scared. And it seems my spark of faith isn't worth the effort. Help me remember that faith as tiny as a mustard seed has power to undo fear. You'll honor my willingness to trust You, no matter how big or small. In Jesus' name I pray, amen.

Because you have so little faith. I tell you this: if you had even a faint spark of faith, even faith as tiny as a mustard seed, you could say to this mountain, "Move from here to there," and because of your faith, the mountain would move. If you had just a sliver of faith, you would find nothing impossible.

MATTHEW 17:20 VOICE

THE FEAR OF BULLIES

Dear God, I'm scared to speak out. I'm afraid of standing up for the right thing. Many are angry and volatile these days, and it feels unsafe to have an opinion. Bullying has become normal, and it keeps me silent. I know the fear is not from You because You promise strength and courage if we ask. Your Word says it's a waste of time to cower to those loud voices because they can't hurt me at the core. They may be rude and spew hateful words, but they can't change who I am in You. And when I ask for confidence to stand strong and say what needs to be said, You'll empower me. Help me remember that! In Jesus' name I pray, amen.

"Don't be bluffed into silence by the threats of bullies. There's nothing they can do to your soul, your core being. Save your fear for God, who holds your entire life— body and soul—in his hands."
MATTHEW 10:28 MSG

COURAGE FOR THE NEXT STEP

Dear God, help me take this next step in faith. I know You're asking me to tread way out of my comfort zone to do something new, and it's terrifying. My heart is anxious at the thought of what's next. I can relate to Esther in today's verses, feeling like there's a possibility for things to go wrong. But like her, I am also fully resolved to follow Your leading. Would You please fill me with courage as I say yes to Your prompting? Shine Your favor on my efforts. Bless me with strategy and creativity. Open the right doors along the way. And give me the courage to take the next step in faith with You. In Jesus' name I pray, amen.

Esther sent back her answer to Mordecai:
"Go and get all the Jews living in Susa together.
Fast for me. Don't eat or drink for three days,
either day or night. I and my maids will fast
with you. If you will do this, I'll go to the king,
even though it's forbidden. If I die, I die."
ESTHER 4:15–16 MSG

NOT AFRAID OF
THE FUTURE

Dear God, let me find peace in knowing You know the details of my life. I don't have to fear the unknown because my future is known. I don't have to be scared because You're already there. What a blessing that I can find rest in Your sovereignty. Thank You for going before me and making plans. That frees me to live in confidence, certain I'll not fall. I believe You have planned peace and not evil for me. That doesn't mean an easy and pain-free life, but it gives hope for the final outcome of my life. It means it will all work out for my benefit and Your glory. I can live with that! In Jesus' name I pray, amen.

For I know the thoughts and plans that I have for you, says the Lord, thoughts and plans for welfare and peace and not for evil, to give you hope in your final outcome.
JEREMIAH 29:11 AMPC

WHEN MONEY CREATES WORRY

Dear God, I get worried about money. I start looking too far into the future, predicting financial ruin. I create stories in my mind of how I'll be unable to make ends meet. It makes me nervous when I try to plan a budget or think about retirement. It feels like money is the god I worship instead of You. When I fixate on money, I take my eyes off You. I forget that You are my source, and I choose to focus on all that could go wrong rather than Your promise to provide and care for me. Forgive me, Lord. Increase my faith so I don't let financial fear rule my day. In Jesus' name I pray, amen.

Keep your lives free from the love of money, and be content with what you have because He has said, "I will never leave you; I will always be by your side." Because of this promise, we may boldly say, The Lord is my help—I won't be afraid of anything. How can anyone harm me?

HEBREWS 13:5–6 VOICE

THE OVERWHELMING FEELINGS OF GRIEF

Dear God, sometimes grief feels so heavy I'm afraid I'll never have peace. I get lost in sadness and hopelessness. And rather than see any light at the end of the tunnel, I just want to curl up in bed and pull the covers over my head. But You're clear in saying that if I choose to keep my mind on You, pressing in for hope and joy, You'll keep me in perfect and constant peace. That means when those worrisome feelings flood my heart and I pray about it, You'll remove the heaviness. It means if I make You my default when grief overwhelms me, the intensity of emotions will be lifted and replaced with peace. In Jesus' name I pray, amen.

You will guard him and keep him in perfect and constant peace whose mind [both its inclination and its character] is stayed on You, because he commits himself to You, leans on You, and hopes confidently in You.

ISAIAH 26:3 AMPC

Overcoming the Fear of Helping Others

Dear God, please fill me with courage to reach out to others who are in need of help. It's so much easier to stay comfortable within my community than to be Your hands and feet to those around me. Maybe it's because I feel ill-equipped. Maybe it's because I'm afraid of messing something up. Maybe it's because I'm worried about my personal safety. Regardless, I could use a dose of divine courage to connect with those in need and show them Your love. Give me the spiritual eyes to see where I can step in and help. Open my heart to being generous with my time. And remove any fear that keeps me tucked away in my comfort zone. In Jesus' name I pray, amen.

This is how we've come to understand and experience love: Christ sacrificed his life for us. This is why we ought to live sacrificially for our fellow believers, and not just be out for ourselves. If you see some brother or sister in need and have the means to do something about it but turn a cold shoulder and do nothing, what happens to God's love? It disappears. And you made it disappear.

1 JOHN 3:16–17 MSG

UNAFRAID TO LOVE YOURSELF

Dear God, I'm not very kind to myself. I criticize and beat myself up on the regular, unable to give myself a break. It seems my expectations are over the top and hold me to a standard I can never live up to. At the root is a worry that I'll never be good enough in the eyes of others, which makes me extra tough on myself. But today's scripture reveals the power of Your love. It tells me that You are greater than my anxious heart. It says You know more about me than I do. And honestly, if You can love me after seeing all my imperfections, certainly I can find the courage to be unafraid to love myself too. In Jesus' name I pray, amen.

My dear children, let's not just talk about love;
let's practice real love. This is the only way we'll
know we're living truly, living in God's reality.
It's also the way to shut down debilitating
self-criticism, even when there is something to it.
For God is greater than our worried hearts and
knows more about us than we do ourselves.
1 JOHN 3:18–20 MSG

Unafraid to Question

Dear God, help me be unafraid to openly question someone's faith when they try to sway me to their mindset. Give me the discernment to know who professes Jesus is Your Son and who does not, because that is the telltale sign of someone who preaches the truth. I'm not supposed to blindly believe everyone. As a matter of fact, Your Word says there will be many false prophets in my day. Help me be quick to discover their true motives. And encourage me to test those who proclaim to follow You. Build my courage and confidence to stand for Your truth rather than cower in acceptance. Fill me with Your wisdom and discernment. In Jesus' name I pray, amen.

Dear friends, don't believe every spirit. Test the spirits to see if they are from God because many false prophets have gone into the world. This is how you know if a spirit comes from God: every spirit that confesses that Jesus Christ has come as a human is from God, and every spirit that doesn't confess Jesus is not from God.

1 John 4:1–3 ceb

No Fear in Leadership

Dear God, I'm in a leadership position, and sometimes I'm frustrated because I feel like I don't have a choice in the matter. I feel thrust into this position—one I didn't really want. I confess that rather than see this as an honor, there are times I complain instead. In my frustration, I can be more of a tyrant than a leader who deeply cares for others' welfare. But I want to change that. Would You transform my mind so I lead by example? Help them know through my words and actions that my heart for them is always good. And take away any fear of leadership and replace it with an eagerness to bring people closer to You. In Jesus' name I pray, amen.

When you shepherd the flock God has given you, watch over them not because you have to but because you want to. For this is how God would want it not because you're being compensated somehow but because you are eager to watch over them. Don't lead them as if you were a dictator, but lead your flock by example.
1 Peter 5:2–3 voice

THE POWER OF TOGETHER

Dear God, give me courage against the enemy. Your Word paints a powerful image of him roaming and looking for someone to devour. Rather than make me afraid, may that visual strengthen me to be alert, knowing his plans are to discourage and distract. With Your help, I can activate my faith and stand strong against him. I may be facing a hard situation, but I'm not alone. There are others facing many of the same circumstances. Somehow that deeply encourages me to resist any and all of the enemy's plans. There is power in numbers! And in You, we have all the power we need as a community of believers to stand strong in faith and be conquerors! In Jesus' name I pray, amen.

Be well balanced and always alert, because your enemy, the devil, roams around incessantly, like a roaring lion looking for its prey to devour. Take a decisive stand against him and resist his every attack with strong, vigorous faith. For you know that your believing brothers and sisters around the world are experiencing the same kinds of troubles you endure.

1 PETER 5:8–9 TPT

THE POWER OF
CLEAR THINKING

Dear God, help me keep my mind clear and use common sense when I start to fear. Give me wisdom to see exactly what's causing the anxiety. Give me discernment to know if my fears are founded in truth or lies. I don't want to waste my one and only life running away and cowering from something that's not real. I don't want to give in to worries that are baseless. Please bless me with spiritual eyes to know the truth so I can live in freedom. Make me strong in my faith as I trust in You to guide and protect me. Build my confidence in who You say I am. And give me courage to brave whatever comes! In Jesus' name I pray, amen.

Dear friend, guard Clear Thinking and Common Sense with your life; don't for a minute lose sight of them. They'll keep your soul alive and well, they'll keep you fit and attractive. You'll travel safely, you'll neither tire nor trip. You'll take afternoon naps without a worry, you'll enjoy a good night's sleep.
PROVERBS 3:21–24 MSG

No Need to Panic

Dear God, when panic begins to set it, my emotions usually spiral out of control. My mind goes in a million different directions as I try to make sense of what's just happened. I struggle to form a clear thought. And rather than take a deep breath, take a step back, and ask You to bring clarity, I end up in a hot mess. When that happens, it's because I've forgotten You are with me in that moment. I've forgotten Your presence enables me to be strong and courageous. I may be caught off guard initially, but my next response should be one of peace and trust. Fear has no hold because trusting You brings peace instead. In Jesus' name I pray, amen.

No need to panic over alarms or surprises,
or predictions that doomsday's just around
the corner, because GOD will be right there
with you; he'll keep you safe and sound.
PROVERBS 3:25–26 MSG

COURAGE IN CHANGES

Dear God, even though Your Word says there are different seasons in life, it's hard for me to accept change. I like comfort and predictability, and I get stirred up when I'm faced with change. It makes me nervous. The unknown is a hard place for me to navigate. Please bring peace to my heart and remind me that You never change. Remind me that there is never a season in life that I'll have to walk through without You. And give me the courage to accept that change is a natural, normal, and good part of life. Even more, make me confident in knowing You're already in those new places making a way for me. In Jesus' name I pray, amen.

For everything that happens in life—
there is a season, a right time for everything
under heaven. . .a time to tear apart, a time
to bind together; a time to be quiet, a time
to speak up; a time to love, a time to hate;
a time to go to war, a time to make peace.

ECCLESIASTES 3:1, 7–8 VOICE

Peace That Calms Anxiety

Dear God, how am I supposed to not worry about things? When my kids are stressing me out and my marriage is on divorce's doorstep, how can I be calm? When I'm falling behind at work and the boss is noticing, how can I rest? When my insecurities overwhelm me and I'm struggling to like myself, how am I supposed to be okay? You say being saturated in prayer is key, but I'm not convinced. Help me give it a shot. Every time fear creeps in, remind me to talk to You about it. Let me share everything down to the minute details of my worry. Show up, Lord. Give me the peace I so desperately need to calm my anxiety. In Jesus' name I pray, amen.

Don't be pulled in different directions or worried about a thing. Be saturated in prayer throughout each day, offering your faith-filled requests before God with overflowing gratitude. Tell him every detail of your life, then God's wonderful peace that transcends human understanding, will guard your heart and mind through Jesus Christ.

Philippians 4:6–7 TPT

THE FEAR OF AGING

Dear God, can I be honest? I know it may sound vain and prideful, but aging scares me. I don't want to watch my body sag. I don't want to deal with wrinkles and a loss of that youthful glow. I want my hair to be full of luster, not silver and thinning. I'm worried about what others will think of me and whether they will judge me based on how time treats me. I need grace for the inevitable process of aging. Shift my perspective so I realize my inner self is full of new life every day. What's more, every day of aging brings me one step closer to an eternity with You. In Jesus' name I pray, amen.

So we have no reason to despair. Despite the fact that our outer humanity is falling apart and decaying, our inner humanity is breathing in new life every day.

2 CORINTHIANS 4:16 VOICE

It's Not Up to You

Dear God, sometimes I put pressure on myself to make everything work out for the best. I decide good and beneficial outcomes depend on my time and effort, so I push to be a playmaker and save the day. It's exhausting. And honestly, all that focus rarely yields the results I was hoping for anyway. There's freedom in remembering that every good and perfect gift comes from You. I don't have to be God because You are. My job is to be obedient to Your leadership and to trust Your will and ways. Anytime I feel afraid or worried that I can't fix or control something, let it be a red flag to surrender it to You. In Jesus' name I pray, amen.

Every good gift, every perfect gift, comes from above. These gifts come down from the Father, the creator of the heavenly lights, in whose character there is no change at all.

James 1:17 CEB

WORRY OVER SPIRITUAL HUNGER

Dear God, Your Word says those who are hungry in the faith are always ready to learn more. They're eager to study and absorb Your truth. They seek You out. But Lord, that's not always me. And it worries me that I'm not always chomping at the bit to read the Bible or spend time with You. I know it's important. I know it's vital to growing in relationship with You. And I feel anxious for not craving it like I think I should. Would You mature that desire in me? I don't want to feel bad any longer; I want to feel inspired to dig into the Bible and deepen my connection to You. In Jesus' name I pray, amen.

The spiritually hungry are always ready to learn more, for their hearts are eager to discover new truths.

PROVERBS 18:15 TPT

THE COURAGE TO WAIT

Dear God, help me be brave as I wait for You. I'm in a tough place right now and desperate for You to intervene. I need to know You will fix this. I need to know You won't leave me stuck in this place. It's hard to sit and wait because my fear gets in the way. I worry that You are too busy, that You have forgotten me, that I'm being punished, or that my expectations of You are too high. I'm surrendering my fears and asking for supernatural patience as I wait for Your plan to unfold in this situation. I'm struggling to stay calm and hold on to peace. Give me courage to sit and wait. In Jesus' name I pray, amen.

Now the Lord is not slow about enacting
His promise—slow is how some people want
to characterize it—no, He is not slow but
patient and merciful to you, not wanting
anyone to be destroyed, but wanting everyone
to turn away from following his own
path and to turn toward God's.

2 PETER 3:9 VOICE

Fear of Being Overlooked

Dear God, I know I'm too concerned with what others think of me. I realize that trying to fit in will only leave me emotionally bankrupt, depressed, and discouraged. But I worry that if I don't make an effort to stay relevant, I won't have any friends. People won't want to include me, and I'll struggle to find community. I'm afraid I'll be overlooked at every turn. You address this struggle, pointing to the value of being transformed from the inside out. Please transform my mind so I'll see my life from the right perspective. Please empower me to see my value and like myself. And please give me discernment to know what is and is not important in life. In Jesus' name I pray, amen.

Stop imitating the ideals and opinions of the culture around you, but be inwardly transformed by the Holy Spirit through a total reformation of how you think. This will empower you to discern God's will as you live a beautiful life, satisfying and perfect in his eyes.

Romans 12:2 tpt

Afraid to Pour Out

Dear God, I am underwater with all the stress in my life. It's one thing after another, and I cannot get on top of my fear and anxiety. Every day, I am struggling to concentrate and focus, and it's too much. Rather than feel hopeful, I battle against complete discouragement. I want to do what the Word says and pour out all my worries and stresses on You, but that's a terrifying proposition. It's such a vulnerable act. And part of me worries it may overwhelm You. Help me trust that You tenderly care for me. Mature my faith to believe it. And grow my courage to override the fear that threatens me. In Jesus' name I pray, amen.

*Pour out all your worries and
stress upon him and leave them there,
for he always tenderly cares for you.*
1 Peter 5:7 tpt

Overcoming
Worrywart Training

Dear God, I come from a long line of worrywarts. As far back as I can remember, my family has been full of anxiety-ridden women, so I come by it innocently. I grew up learning to be afraid of everything. I was taught to expect the worst in others and predict horrible outcomes in situations. There was always something to be concerned about. That cup-half-empty mindset has followed me into adulthood, and I am ready to be free from it. Help me live in freedom and with hope, knowing You will fulfill every promise to take care of my every need. I don't have to live in fear or defeat because You won't let me fall. In Jesus' name I pray, amen.

Here is the bottom line: do not worry about your life. Don't worry about what you will eat or what you will drink. Don't worry about how you clothe your body. Living is about more than merely eating, and the body is about more than dressing up.
Matthew 6:25 voice

The God of Small Details

Dear God, the depth of Your love is obvious. There is nothing that escapes Your eye. Not one living being goes unnoticed. From me down to the birds, You show care and concern for us all. Every time I begin to worry about the smallest details of my day, remind me that You are the God of small details. Fill me with courage to trust that You see the unmentioned needs buried deep in my pain. Encourage me to share every worry or fear no matter how insignificant they seem to me, knowing they are not insignificant to You. What a gift to be seen and known by the One who created me. In Jesus' name I pray, amen.

Look at the birds in the sky. They do not store food for winter. They don't plant gardens. They do not sow or reap—and yet, they are always fed because your heavenly Father feeds them. And you are even more precious to Him than a beautiful bird. If He looks after them, of course He will look after you.

Matthew 6:26 voice

WHEN WORRY SUBTRACTS

Dear God, I know that worrying subtracts in my life. It robs and steals from me. It rips away things like peace and harmony. And it leaves a gaping hole in my heart that I can't seem to fill on my own. Looking back, I realize there's never been a time when my worrying accomplished anything good. It has never tweaked the outcome for the better or made me feel stronger in the moment. Instead, anxiety has worked against me. So let this revelation be what drives me to You for help and encouragement every time. Be a powerful and settling force in my life. Restore my peace and hope, and let me find rest in You. In Jesus' name I pray, amen.

Worrying does not do any good;
who here can claim to add even
an hour to his life by worrying?
MATTHEW 6:27 VOICE

STARVING FEAR

Dear God, when Your Word tells me to let the things of tomorrow worry about themselves, it sounds like a command to starve the fear they bring. It's choosing not to let anxiety have any playtime. It's like closing the door to an unwanted solicitor demanding my resources. So the next time I begin to worry about my children's futures based on their current choices, I'm going to shut that worry down. I won't go down the rabbit hole of fear about my health, especially without any diagnosis. I won't forecast a terrible retirement based on today's market report. Instead, help me be present here and now, walking out my faith with a sense of peace. In Jesus' name I pray, amen.

So do not worry about tomorrow.
Let tomorrow worry about itself. Living
faithfully is a large enough task for today.
MATTHEW 6:34 VOICE

Speak Hopefulness

Dear God, every time I'm afraid or bogged down by the worries of the day, I'm going to speak hopefulness. I'm going to use my voice to declare Your goodness rather than whimper and crumble under the weight of stress. If I'm scared, I will declare courage. If I'm stressed, I will declare peace. If I'm overwhelmed, I will declare strength. Let the words I say be an encouragement to my soul. I won't stay quiet when my ears need to hear a cheerful and faith-filled word. Help me stay positive. Remind me that I am a victor. And increase my faith to navigate the weary times, knowing You always promise a way out. In Jesus' name I pray, amen.

Worry weighs us down;
a cheerful word picks us up.
Proverbs 12:25 msg

THE TRUTH OF CHRIST

Dear God, the Word says I can have strength for every single thing because Jesus empowers me. It's through Him that I can overcome fear. He is the reason I don't get pulled under by stress and strife. I am ready for anything because of Him. But I don't feel that way right now. In this moment, I'm terrified by the situations I'm facing. I am tired of every day bringing a new set of anxieties. I am feeling rather hopeless that my life can ever change. And if You don't shift that mindset in me, I'm worried I'll be stuck here forever. Please help me stand strong in the truth of Christ. I need Your help. In Jesus' name I pray, amen.

I have strength for all things in Christ Who empowers me [I am ready for anything and equal to anything through Him Who infuses inner strength into me; I am self-sufficient in Christ's sufficiency].

PHILIPPIANS 4:13 AMPC

GO TO GOD

Dear God, I will absolutely take You up on the offer extended in today's verse. I'm coming to You overwhelmed and weary and tired, and I need the kind of rest only You can provide. I'm done trying to fix things myself because I just make them worse. The world has done me no favor except to fray my nerves. And what I really want is to climb into Your lap and cry. I want Your voice to soothe me and Your peace to overwhelm me. I don't like the way the world has treated me, and I need a break. It's been a tough season on so many levels. Help me find relief and refreshment in Your presence. In Jesus' name I pray, amen.

Come to Me, all you who labor and are heavy-laden and overburdened, and I will cause you to rest. [I will ease and relieve and refresh your souls.]
MATTHEW 11:28 AMPC

THE DIVINE EXCHANGE

Dear God, teach me to be unafraid. This world breeds fear because it's cruel and demanding. It overexpects and underdelivers. And it has created a fearful heart in me. Too often, I look to others for comfort. I take my brokenness into the world and ask for solutions. I put all my hope for help and healing into incapable hands—including my own. But the Word says You're gentle and humble. It promises rest for me from the cares and fears of the world. And You'll exchange my heavy burden for a yoke that is easy and light instead. I don't have to be afraid because You promise peace. Anytime I begin looking to the world, bring me back to You. In Jesus' name I pray, amen.

"Put on my yoke, and learn from me. I'm gentle and humble. And you will find rest for yourselves. My yoke is easy to bear, and my burden is light."
MATTHEW 11:29–30 CEB

At His Feet

Dear God, I've got nothing left in me. My heart is heavy, and I have no energy to carry on. I'm so afraid that my deepest fears will come true and I won't be able to stop them. My resolve to fight back is gone, and I just want to give up because the weight of my worry is too much to bear. When You tell me to leave all my cares and anxieties at Your feet, can I trust You with them? I want to, but there's a control issue inside me that needs to know for sure. Mature my faith so I can be confident to let go and let You replace those fears with grace and strength. In Jesus' name I pray, amen.

So here's what I've learned through it all: Leave all your cares and anxieties at the feet of the Lord, and measureless grace will strengthen you.

Psalm 55:22 TPT

When It's Hard to Trust God with Your Needs

Dear God, it seems that too often I look everywhere else for my needs to be met except to You. When my feelings get hurt, I run to my friends and unpack the situation, looking for comfort through their words. When I'm worried about money, I fret in solitude because I don't want to be judged by others. In those scary seasons of parenting when I feel I'm failing, I turn to food, alcohol, and other numbing agents. I don't want to live this way anymore because it means I am missing out on the awesome display of Your power to answer every need I may have. So Lord, today I am choosing to surrender my needs to You. In Jesus' name I pray, amen.

My God will meet your every need
out of his riches in the glory that
is found in Christ Jesus.
Philippians 4:19 CEB

WHEN WE NEED
OUR OWN MOSES

Dear God, I'm humbly asking You to bless me with a Moses in my own life. I need someone who will not only encourage me when I'm struggling but also be quick to challenge me to take the next right step in faith when I feel unable. So often I need to be reminded that You're always with me, guiding each step I take. And like Joshua, there are times I need a bold voice to readjust my focus on that truth. I want someone who believes in me and loves You! So Lord, please bring me a Moses. And even more, give me a willing heart to listen to and accept that person's wisdom. In Jesus' name I pray, amen.

[Moses said to Joshua,] Be strong and brave! You're going to lead these people into the land the Eternal promised their ancestors He'd give them. You'll give it to them, and they'll give it to their descendants. And He will be leading you. He'll be with you, and He'll never fail you or abandon you. So don't be afraid!

DEUTERONOMY 31:7–8 VOICE

THE CALL TO ENCOURAGE ONE ANOTHER

Dear God, I don't have many good friends who encourage me to be strong. Honestly, everyone is battling their own stuff right now. We're all eyeball deep in it. So rather than rely on community for a vote of confidence, I give in to fear and shut down. But God, I want what today's verse reveals. I want friendships where we help one another navigate the tricky situations life brings. There's great value in having someone believe in you—that you have what it takes to get to the other side of the mess. So Lord, in Your kindness and love, help me find friendships where I can encourage and be encouraged. It'll be a game changer. In Jesus' name I pray, amen.

Each helps the other, each saying
to the other, "Take courage!"
ISAIAH 41:6 CEB

GOD WILL VINDICATE

Dear God, today I choose to hand You my hurt and anger. I'm setting aside my plans for revenge. I'm confessing my battle with fear, and I'm deciding to let go of my tendency to obsess about what offends me. Instead, I'm going to trust that You have seen every injustice that's come my way and will respond to each one at the right time and in Your righteous way. It's not my place to play God, and I confess all the times I have. Thank You for caring about me and knowing those moments when fear fills my heart. Even more, thank You for promising to vindicate me so I don't get tangled in sin as I plot and plan. In Jesus' name I pray, amen.

"All who rage against you will be ashamed and disgraced. All who contend with you will perish and disappear. You will look for your enemies in vain; those who war against you will vanish without a trace!"

ISAIAH 41:11–12 TPT

Count on God

Dear God, my heart is anxious about so many things right now. I'm battling anxiety on epic levels and just can't seem to find a sustainable sense of peace. I am bogged down by feelings of dread. No doubt, this season of life has been extremely difficult, especially with so many things coming at me from every direction. I just feel hopeless, like nothing is going to change. Please hold me tight and let me feel Your presence. Please calm my anxious heart. Be quick to show me the way to peace, and give me courage to walk that path. I can't seem to find my way out of this valley, and I'm counting on You to rescue me. In Jesus' name I pray, amen.

"That's right. Because I, your God, have a firm grip on you and I'm not letting go. I'm telling you, 'Don't panic. I'm right here to help you.' "

Isaiah 41:13 msg

RELEASE CONTROL

Dear God, help me release the steering wheel so You can be in the driver's seat of my life. Give me courage to step aside so You have complete freedom to lead and I feel comfortable with following. I realize that having control is my way of attempting to manage the things that scare me. But when I hold on and try to power my way through in my own strength and wisdom, I only end up deeper in stress. Thank You for offering to be my Guide through the hard times. Today I happily and officially surrender to Your leading. Give me the courage to trust that You always have my best in mind. In Jesus' name I pray, amen.

Then Jesus went to work on his disciples. "Anyone who intends to come with me has to let me lead. You're not in the driver's seat; I am."
MATTHEW 16:24 MSG

Embrace Suffering

Dear God, the idea of embracing suffering absolutely terrifies me. What if I stop fighting and it wins? What if it overtakes me and I lose myself? What if I develop a victim mentality and it alienates me from my friends and family? But since Your Word says to embrace suffering, there must be a good reason. Maybe it's because when we fight against something, so often it's in self-defense. It's in our own strength and for self-preservation. If You're asking me to trust You with hard seasons instead, then make me brave. Increase my confidence in Your sovereignty. Teach me how to surrender my will to Yours. And help me shift my perspective so I can trust You over me. In Jesus' name I pray, amen.

"Don't run from suffering; embrace it.
Follow me and I'll show you how. Self-help
is no help at all. Self-sacrifice is the way,
my way, to finding yourself, your true self."
MATTHEW 16:25 MSG

Look at Jesus

Dear God, help me keep my eyes only on You when I'm afraid. When I'm in scary or uncomfortable situations, keep me from staring at the circumstances that are overwhelming me. I'm tired of living in fear. The reality is I've spent too much time letting my Goliaths knock me off balance in the past. I've given them too much power over my heart. I've entertained them too long in my mind. And the only thing that has done is rob me of joy and peace. I confess these giants have become bigger than You too often. So thank You for Jesus. He is the answer. He's the One who came for freedom. Let me keep my eyes only on Him. In Jesus' name I pray, amen.

When they opened their eyes and looked around all they saw was Jesus, only Jesus.
MATTHEW 17:8 MSG

Looking past Charisma

Dear God, I don't want to be easily swayed into believing the wrong things. Sometimes I feel naive and am confused by the charisma of others. Some people can be so persuasive! So please keep me from falling prey to false teachers or ungodly role models. Instead, anchor me in You, Lord. Bolster my confidence in the relationship I have with You so I'm not fearful of falling for the wrong thing. Let me be quick to question something that doesn't sit right in my spirit. Give me Your wisdom and discernment to know the difference between truth and lies. And fill me with courage to stand up for what I know is right. In Jesus' name I pray, amen.

See to it that nobody enslaves you with philosophy and foolish deception, which conform to human traditions and the way the world thinks and acts rather than Christ.

Colossians 2:8 ceb

YOUR DEBT IS DESTROYED

Dear God, don't let my heart be worried about the consequences of sin. Because Jesus is my personal Savior and I believe He is Your Son, remind me that His death on the cross took care of every bad choice—past, present, and future. I don't have to live in fear that lightning will strike me or that I'll spend eternity in hell as punishment. It's because of Jesus I can live confidently, trusting that my sin debt has been paid in full. The ledger is balanced. Help me embrace the freedom that comes from a relationship with You, Lord! And make me fearless as I trust You over any fear the enemy tries to stir up in my spirit. In Jesus' name I pray, amen.

*He destroyed the record of the debt we owed,
with its requirements that worked against us.
He canceled it by nailing it to the cross.*

COLOSSIANS 2:14 CEB

Being Their Advocate

Dear God, give me courage to be bold in my advocacy of others. Help me stand strong for those who feel too weak to stand for themselves. Help me speak for those who are afraid, whose voices have been silenced. What we think and feel matters! Would You give me eyes to see the vulnerable and help me meet them with compassion? Fill my heart with love for the needy and poor. I don't want to be afraid to advocate when it's necessary. I don't want to be afraid to be Your hands and feet in the world. Strengthen me to defend anyone You put on my heart. And give me confidence in You that can't be shaken by insecurity. In Jesus' name I pray, amen.

Speak out on behalf of the voiceless, and for the rights of all who are vulnerable. Speak out in order to judge with righteousness and to defend the needy and the poor.
Proverbs 31:8–9 CEB

Fear of Never Being Good Enough

Dear God, I have such a fear of never being good enough. It's something that's been with me for as far back as I can remember. So many people have reiterated it through the years that I've adopted it as truth. Wrapping my brain around the fact that You fully accept me is hard to do. Knowing You've folded me into Your family is a powerful revelation I'm trying to grab onto. Believing I will never be alone or abandoned feels foreign. But Father, I want all these truths to be settled in my spirit. I want them to be alive in me. And I don't want the fear of falling short to have any room to grow anymore. In Jesus' name I pray, amen.

And you did not receive the "spirit of religious duty," leading you back into the fear of never being good enough. But you have received the "Spirit of full acceptance," enfolding you into the family of God. And you will never feel orphaned, for as he rises up within us, our spirits join him in saying the words of tender affection, "Beloved Father!"
ROMANS 8:15 TPT

My Bubble of Predictability

Dear God, stepping out of my comfort zone is terrifying. I like the safety of my bubble of predictability because I'm in control there. So the idea of changing things and doing something new feels out of control. I don't like it. But Your Word says that no matter where I go, You are with me. It says You will watch over me and stay close always. Would You increase my faith so I can have steadfast confidence in these promises? I want to live in faith, trusting You for my next step. And if that means I step out of the bubble and into something new, give me the courage to follow where You lead. In Jesus' name I pray, amen.

Know I am with you, and I will watch over you no matter where you go. One day I will bring you back to this land. I will not leave you until I have done all I have promised you.
Genesis 28:15 voice

Please Be Big

Dear God, sometimes I don't know what to do next. I freeze up in my fear, scared to stand still or make a move. It's confusing and frustrating at the same time. In those times when I feel helpless, please be big. I don't always know how to pray or what to ask for, but You know exactly what to do. I trust that You will intervene at the right time and in the right way. I believe in my heart that You are mighty to save and always have my best in mind. So please help me. Respond to my hopelessness and grow my confidence in Your love and protection. I am looking to You alone. In Jesus' name I pray, amen.

"O dear God, won't you take care of them?
We're helpless before this vandal horde
ready to attack us. We don't know what
to do; we're looking to you."
2 Chronicles 20:12 msg

WHEN TO BATTLE AND WHEN TO WATCH

Dear God, sometimes I don't know when I'm to engage in the battle and when You are the One who will take the lead on my behalf. I don't want to get in the way or make things worse, so please help me discern my role in the situation. I don't want to react out of fear and jump into the mix when Your plan is for me to stand ready and watch the way You deliver me from the battle. In the same vein, don't let me cower when the plan is for me to advocate for myself. I need Your wisdom and strength to guide me in the right ways. In Jesus' name I pray, amen.

"You don't need to fight this battle. Just take your places, stand ready, and watch how the LORD, who is with you, will deliver you, Judah and Jerusalem. Don't be afraid or discouraged! Go out tomorrow and face them. The LORD will be with you."
2 CHRONICLES 20:17 CEB

But We Have the Lord

Dear God, help me be fearless because I know You are always with me. In those moments when I want to cower, give me courage. When I feel intimidated, make me brave. When I begin to crumble in my own strength, remind me that You are with me, fighting! Life may look overwhelming from my human perspective. I may feel small in relation to the Goliath in front of me. My situation may threaten and taunt me with hopelessness. But when I put my trust in You, Lord, all the power of heaven is backing me up. Let this be my battle cry as I walk through the ups and downs of life. Let this be why I can stand fearless! In Jesus' name I pray, amen.

*"All he has is human strength,
but we have the Lord our God,
who will help us fight our battles!"*
2 Chronicles 32:8 CEB

HE IS YOUR FRIEND

Dear God, thank You for being my best friend. Thank You for wanting to be invested in my life in meaningful ways. I'm so grateful that You promise to shepherd my heart as I walk through life. Let these truths sink deep in me, giving me courage and confidence that I can overcome anything that stands in my way. Knowing I'll always have more than enough of whatever it is that I need through Your generosity encourages me to stay strong through the storms of life. I know You will be faithful to equip me. You will defend my heart. You will bless my life. And that means there is no fear that can overtake me. In Jesus' name I pray, amen.

Yahweh is my best friend and my shepherd.
I always have more than enough.
PSALM 23:1 TPT

Finding Rest

Dear God, I'm desperate for rest. The battle has been so intense lately, filling me with all kinds of fear. It has exhausted me because I am always on guard, always hypervigilant of what's going on around me. My heart is full of anxiety, and I'm worried about all sorts of things that could go wrong. What's more, I don't see any relief in sight. Please give me peace. Please soothe my fears as You restore me. I am too weak, Lord, and I'm asking You to straighten the crooked paths I'm on right now. Bring me out of the chaos and help me steady my gaze on You. Fill me with confidence that with You I will always find rest! In Jesus' name I pray, amen.

He provides me rest in rich, green fields beside streams of refreshing water. He soothes my fears; He makes me whole again, steering me off worn, hard paths to roads where truth and righteousness echo His name.

PSALM 23:2–3 VOICE

THOSE UNENDING SHADOWS

Dear God, sometimes it seems I'm disappearing into the unending shadows surrounding me. Right now, I'm fighting to navigate what feels like darkness in some of the relationships that mean the most to me. I'm worried about losing people I love, scared they may walk away from me. I feel like I can't do anything right in their eyes, and it seems we're always at odds. It's this instability that scares me because I don't want to lose them. Please put a hedge of protection around me. Guide me into truth and show me the next step. You are a good God, and I trust You to shine a light so the unending shadows are no longer an issue. In Jesus' name I pray, amen.

Even in the unending shadows of death's darkness, I am not overcome by fear. Because You are with me in those dark moments, near with Your protection and guidance, I am comforted.

PSALM 23:4 VOICE

A Massive Meal
in Front of Them

Dear God, I can't help but giggle at the thought of You serving me a massive meal as my enemies sit and watch. It will be me sitting in plenty, thanks to Your hand. I will be the one receiving the blessing of abundance, not them. It will be my chin that's lifted, a signal that fear and hurt are fading away. What a beautiful picture of Your love! And honestly, I'm so grateful to know You see all the wrongs against me. You know who set themselves as my enemies. You understand the situations that cause me to be afraid and anxious. I never have to worry about things being unseen. Thank You! In Jesus' name I pray, amen.

You serve me a six-course dinner right in front of my enemies. You revive my drooping head; my cup brims with blessing.
Psalm 23:5 msg

YOU ARE PURSUED

Dear God, I love knowing You pursue me now and always will. It calms my heart to realize there's nothing I can do to make You walk away from me. I can't sin too much. I'll never run out of second chances with You. And there's a hope-filled future waiting for me. So when I begin to project negativity about how tomorrow may look, remind me that Your heart for me is good. Whisper into my spirit that Your love never fails. Breathe joy and peace into my soul, giving me courage to stay the course in faith. And never let me forget that once my race on earth is done, I will spend forever in Your glorious presence. In Jesus' name I pray, amen.

So why would I fear the future? Only goodness and love pursue me all the days of my life. Then afterward, when my life is through, I'll return to your glorious presence to be forever with you!
PSALM 23:6 TPT

God Listens to You

Dear God, please hear what's on my heart. Even when the words don't come out right, or don't come out at all, hear me. Know the intimate details of every fear that has me tangled in knots. See the heaviness of thought that's on my mind right now. Feel the weighty insecurities that are keeping me from standing up for myself. And understand the reasons I am paralyzed and unable to make decisions. I'm a mess and desperate for the sweet relief only You can bring. I simply cannot take the next step because I lack courage. My confidence is shot, and I'm not sure of my next move. Please help me, Lord. I'm waiting. In Jesus' name I pray, amen.

I am passionately in love with God because he listens to me. He hears my prayers and answers them. As long as I live I'll keep praying to him, for he stoops down to listen to my heart's cry.

Psalm 116:1–2 TPT

Kind and Gracious

Dear God, some of my favorite things about You are the kindness and graciousness You've shown me. Whether I'm dancing high on a mountaintop or dragging myself though a dark valley, You hear me. You see me. And I can remember countless times You've reached down from heaven and saved me. In strength, You doused my fear so it didn't own me. With Your help, worry never consumed me—at least not for long. You made me brave when I felt anything but. I see the value in looking back at Your track record in my life, remembering every single time You showed up. Thank You for those memories. Bring them to mind anytime I need encouragement. In Jesus' name I pray, amen.

I cried out to the Lord, "God, come and save me!" He was so kind, so gracious to me. Because of his passion toward me, he made everything right and he restored me.

Psalm 116:4–5 tpt

THE POWER OF PRAISE

Dear God, I know there's power in praise. It has a beautiful way of lightening the heavy load I'm carrying. Recognizing Your greatness builds up unshakable confidence in my spirit. It quickly melts away fear that keeps me stuck, unable to move forward. When I choose to focus on Your goodness instead of my messiness, I feel a surge of hope deep in my heart. Yes, I know I'm deeply loved by You! Help me remember to praise You in the storm as I wait for You to rescue me. When I'm feeling down, move me to count all the ways You have been big in my life. When things feel overwhelming, point me to the Word for unmatched encouragement. In Jesus' name I pray, amen.

Praise God, everybody! Applaud God,
all people! His love has taken over our lives;
God's faithful ways are eternal. Hallelujah!
PSALM 117:1–2 MSG

His Love Never Quits

Dear God, thank You that Your love never quits. I'm grateful that no matter what, You'll never give up on me. In a world where love feels shallow and conditional, what a relief to know Yours never is. And it's Your love that helps me conquer fear. I know the promises packed into the love You offer, and they steady me when life feels overwhelming. I can always go back to You with my heartbreak and fear because Your love never fails to meet me right where I am. I will stand strong because You straighten my back with confidence. And in those times when I forget these things, rush in a reminder so I feel courageous to press on! In Jesus' name I pray, amen.

Thank GOD because he's good, because his love never quits. Tell the world, Israel, "His love never quits." And you, clan of Aaron, tell the world, "His love never quits." And you who fear GOD, join in, "His love never quits."

PSALM 118:1–4 MSG

GOD IS YOUR FATHER

Dear God, be my Father right now. Fill the void my earthly father left in my life. Teach me all the things he should have taught me. My heart aches for the father I needed and wanted but didn't get. There are deep wounds and fears he left in my heart—places exposed and unhealed. Please open my eyes to see all the ways You're filling that gap. Let me know You're making up the difference. The pain I've experienced because my earthly father failed me is extensive. But You, Lord, have rescued me without fail. You've been faithful to calm my anxiousness and begin healing my insecurities. And I'm so grateful You are my Father. In Jesus' name I pray, amen.

Out of my deep anguish and pain I prayed, and God, you helped me as a father. You came to my rescue and broke open the way into a beautiful and broad place. Now I know, Lord, that you are for me, and I will never fear what man can do to me.

PSALM 118:5–6 TPT

TRUSTING GOD OVER PEOPLE

Dear God, help me break the lifelong habit of putting my trust in people. Not only do I eventually feel let down or abandoned, but it's not fair to them either. They're not my savior, and thinking they are sets them up for failure. By design, they aren't that powerful. I don't want to continue looking to my friends and family to rescue me. I don't want to tax them with my struggles or come off as too needy. Instead, let me remember to bring my fears and frustrations directly to You because You'll never see me as too much. I won't ever be too needy in Your eyes. My faith is in You. In Jesus' name I pray, amen.

It is better to put your faith in the Eternal
for your security than to trust in people.
It is better to put your faith in Him for
your security than to trust in princes.
PSALM 118:8–9 VOICE

THE GOOD OF BEING TESTED

Dear God, I know that sometimes the only way I'll learn is to be tested. The only way I'll grow in my faith is to be put in situations where I have to flex those muscles that easily atrophy. But I'll be honest, I'm not a fan of these times. They stir up fear and insecurity. They trigger memories of heartbreak, leaving me sad. My anger flares up from frustrating circumstances. But Lord, I know it's because of love that You allow me to endure this kind of testing. I know it's used as a tool to deepen my level of trust. You push me to grow me, and I'm grateful for the confidence boost. In Jesus' name I pray, amen.

I didn't die. I lived! And now I'm telling the world what God did. God tested me, he pushed me hard, but he didn't hand me over to Death.
PSALM 118:17–18 MSG

Can't Outlast His Love

Dear God, I know fear isn't stronger than You. It can't outlast or outblast Your love. Anxiety crumbles the moment I bring You into the mix. I can't even count the number of times I've seen this happen in my life. But there are moments when I still forget this truth that I need to know without fail. This information is life changing. Your love has the power to bring healing and hope to the things that threaten to drain every ounce of my courage. Lord, please help me grab onto You every time I feel afraid. I don't want to give in to fear ever again. Instead, I want to bask in Your glory and goodness—forever! In Jesus' name I pray, amen.

So let's keep on giving our thanks
to God, for he is so good! His constant,
tender love lasts forever!
Psalm 118:29 TPT

THAT KIND OF COURAGE

Dear God, when I read about what Your Son went through to pay for my sin and bridge the gap it left between me and You, I'm in awe. From my human viewpoint, I would have been so afraid to face it. I would have begged for a way out to avoid the pain and humiliation. But He never wavered in the reason He came to earth. Jesus had an eye on His purpose. And if there was any fear to speak of, it never interfered. Give me that kind of courage. Let me approach hard things in that way. Allow my steadfastness to show as I rise up in bravery regardless of what comes my way. In Jesus' name I pray, amen.

He was oppressed and harshly mistreated;
still he humbly submitted, refusing to defend
himself. He was brought like a gentle lamb to
be slaughtered. Like a silent sheep before his
shearers, he didn't even open his mouth.
ISAIAH 53:7 TPT

THE SILVER LINING

Dear God, it's hard to imagine that my troubles and struggles have a silver lining. Where I only see them as a mess, You see the whole picture. They may feel like doom and gloom to me, but there is great purpose in the trials I face. And when I only see a Goliath, You already know the outcome of the battle. I need Your perspective. Let me peek behind the curtain so I can find the courage to battle on. Help me be fearless as I trust You in my circumstances. Help me be positive rather than shrivel up in fear and worry. Help me see the purpose, and bless me with confidence in You! In Jesus' name I pray, amen.

I have good news, brothers and sisters;
and I want to share it. Believe it or not,
my imprisonment has actually helped spread
the good news to new places and populations.

PHILIPPIANS 1:12 VOICE

INSPIRED BY OVERCOMERS

Dear God, there is nothing more encouraging than watching someone stand strong during tough seasons of life. It gives me strength for what's ahead and helps me feel hopeful that everything will be okay. When I want to give in and bury my head in the sand, remembering the testimony of an overcomer spurs me on. Lord, let me be that for others. Let my story be what inspires someone else to stay positive and hopeful. Keep me focused on Your goodness every time fear threatens to steal my peace. Whether I'm scared because of a diagnosis, a bill, an argument, or something else, with Your help I can be fearless and resolved. In Jesus' name I pray, amen.

Not only that, but most of the followers of Jesus here have become far more sure of themselves in the faith than ever, speaking out fearlessly about God, about the Messiah.
PHILIPPIANS 1:14 MSG

VICTORY FOR GOOD REASON

Dear God, the victory through You over my debilitating fear matters for lots of reasons. It puts the spotlight on Your awesomeness and might. It points to endless possibilities as I trust in You. And it shows the power of prayer. Even more, my freedom from fear highlights You as a Healer. For so long, I tried to figure out my problems on my own. I am capable! But I discovered that my own strength had huge limitations, and I wasn't able to be my own savior for long. I couldn't squash the fear that had a tight grip on me. But You came through for me time and time again. And I give You the glory! In Jesus' name I pray, amen.

"But I've left you standing for this reason:
in order to show you my power and in order
to make my name known in the whole world."

EXODUS 9:16 CEB

THE CHALLENGE OF GOOD COURAGE

Dear God, I know Your desire is for me to respond with courage at every turn. I know that when it feels impossible to be brave, I can find bravery through You. And I understand how important it is for others to see a healthy level of confidence from me because it helps them feel confident too. But there are times I just want to hide instead. Sometimes it just feels too overwhelming and I've lost my gumption to fight on. It's in those times I am desperate for hope. This is when I need others to come alongside me with reassurance and encouragement. This is when I need You to intervene with supernatural strength and confidence. In Jesus' name I pray, amen.

Be of good courage and let us behave ourselves courageously for our people and for the cities of our God; and may the Lord do what is good in His sight.

1 CHRONICLES 19:13 AMPC

GOD GETS ALL THE GLORY

Dear God, thank You for being my Rescuer and Protector. So often, I come to You with all my fears and troubles. And while I know that's okay, right now I just want to recognize the awesomeness of who You are. I want to acknowledge all the ways You've blessed me over the years. I want to give every bit of the glory to You for the faithfulness that's been shown to me. Your trustworthiness has healed some places in me where I've experienced betrayal and abandonment from others. And when my fear has taken hold of me, You have been my rescuing knight every single time. Today God, all the glory is Yours. I love You. In Jesus' name I pray, amen.

Blessed be GOD, my mountain, who trains me to fight fair and well. He's the bedrock on which I stand, the castle in which I live, my rescuing knight, the high crag where I run for dear life, while he lays my enemies low.

PSALM 144:1–2 MSG

A Fierce Protector

Dear God, can I be honest? I'm asking You to vindicate me in big ways—visible ways. I need You to storm out of heaven on my behalf and fight for me. I'm too afraid to battle on my own because I'm unskilled, but You are my Protector. And I'm asking You to be fierce. Can You see me down here cowering in fear, drowning in the ocean of hate that's pulling me under? Please save me. Please pull me from this scary situation and instill courage in my heart. Let me witness You battling all that's come against me. It will do my heart some good to see justice and mercy lean in my direction. In Jesus' name I pray, amen.

Step down out of heaven, GOD; ignite volcanoes in the hearts of the mountains. Hurl your lightnings in every direction; shoot your arrows this way and that. Reach all the way from sky to sea: pull me out of the ocean of hate, out of the grip of those barbarians who lie through their teeth, who shake your hand then knife you in the back.

PSALM 144:5–8 MSG

When Surrounded by Lies

Dear God, I am surrounded by people who are full of lies. They spin everything in their favor, and it goes against what I know to be real and true. It goes against You and morality, and I can't stand it. I feel trapped because if I challenge them, there will be retribution, and that thought produces so much fear in my heart. So either I keep my mouth shut and let frustration build or I speak out and risk their wrath. Would You give me courage and wisdom in spades right now? Would You open my eyes to see the path You're illuminating for me to walk? I am so confused and need help. In Jesus' name I pray, amen.

Deliver me and save me from these
dark powers who speak nothing but lies.
Their words are pure deceit, and you
can't trust anything they say.

Psalm 144:11 tpt

A BLESSING

Dear God, let today's scripture be a blessing for me. With all that I've endured in this season, I'm asking You to make this my reality. These past few months have been so heavy. I'm feeling overwhelmed with all that life has been throwing my way. Lord, I need a break. My biggest fear is that nothing will change. I'm terrified my current situation will be forever. And I just don't have the strength to go on. I can't continue this way any longer, exhausted from the battle and angry that I feel stuck. Rescue me and restore me to a bountiful life full of examples of Your goodness. Let me breathe fresh air in Your presence. In Jesus' name I pray, amen.

Our barns will be filled to the brim, overflowing with the fruits of our harvest. Our fields will be full of sheep and cattle, too many to count, and our livestock will not miscarry their young. Our enemies will not invade our land, and there'll be no breach in our walls.
PSALM 144:13–14 TPT

117

Don't Be Afraid
to Advocate

Dear God, don't let my fear of rejection keep me from being an advocate for others. Although I struggle with some deep insecurities, don't let them stand in my way of speaking up for those who need help the most. I want to be Your hands and feet to the world, letting nothing stop me from loving the disenfranchised. Use me in mighty ways to bring hope and encouragement. Let my words and actions reassure them that they are loved by You. Boost my confidence so I can do the job You've placed before me. And Lord, fill my heart with passion and my life with purpose for Your people. Give me the courage necessary to inspire them. In Jesus' name I pray, amen.

"Stand up for the poor and the orphan; advocate for the rights of the afflicted and those in need. Deliver the poor and the needy; rescue them from their evil oppressors."
PSALM 82:3–4 VOICE

Everything and Everyone

Dear God, when I'm feeling afraid and worried about life, remind me that You are in complete control. The whole world is in Your capable hands, so there is nothing I should fear. Nothing is bigger than You. So let that powerful fact give me the courage I need to believe I am covered by You, especially when I feel scared. Let it be what reinforces my confidence that nothing escapes Your gaze—not even for a moment. Let it support my deepest hope that good things will happen and truth will always prevail. For You are the Judge who presides over everything and everyone. And because I am Yours, I'm in good hands. In Jesus' name I pray, amen.

All rise! For God now takes his place as judge of all the earth. Don't you know that everything and everyone belongs to him? The nations will be sifted in his hands!

PSALM 82:8 TPT

LIVE WITHOUT FEAR

Dear God, in the Bible You are clear. You tell us in one form or another not to fear over three hundred times. Since it's something You speak about often, that tells me it's something You're very passionate about. You must have known humankind would struggle with fear. Maybe that's why You call us so strongly to have courage and faith. But Lord, I have lived with fear for so long. It's been a constant companion throughout my life, and I'm realizing it's also the lens through which I make decisions. I'm not even sure how to live without it. Free me from its hold. Would You please remove the power it has on me? In Jesus' name I pray, amen.

Do not fear them or their words, son of man.
Though you will dwell among the thistles
and briars of their hostility, though their
reactions will make you think you're sitting on
scorpions, do not be afraid. Pay no attention to
their threats, and don't let their glaring faces
intimidate you. They are a rebellious lot.

EZEKIEL 2:6 VOICE

Don't Stay Silent

Dear God, whenever I begin to shut down, help me see it. Sometimes my insecurities keep me from sharing my faith and testimony. I cower without even realizing it. I get scared to open up about my relationship with You. I worry about what others might think; then I lose confidence and stay silent. But Lord, I've seen You do amazing things in my life. I've had a front-row seat as You've healed, restored, and saved me. I don't want to stay quiet about these things. Make me brave to honestly share all the ways You've loved me. It's worthy of celebration! And what's more, it may be the boost needed to grow someone's faith in You. In Jesus' name I pray, amen.

"It's impossible for us to stop speaking about all the things we've seen and heard!"
ACTS 4:20 TPT

Shake, Shake, Shake

Dear God, rather than let my fears shake me, let my prayers shake heaven and earth! Let me pray with such power and strength that it destabilizes the things trying to weaken me. Let me be quick to bring my worries directly to You, full of hope and expectation for relief. I know the world can be scary. It's full of people and situations that threaten my resolve to trust You. And while I'll face moments when I feel weak, the Holy Spirit makes me strong! I am fortified though my belief in You, Lord. Continue building my faith so I can stand in courage and confidence even when my life feels knocked off balance. In Jesus' name I pray, amen.

They finished their prayer, and immediately the whole place where they had gathered began to shake. All the disciples were filled with the Holy Spirit, and they began speaking God's message with courageous confidence.

Acts 4:31 voice

FEAR IN LEADERSHIP

Dear God, I don't know how Joshua did it. In a moment, he was called up. He was thrown into leadership without any choice but to obey. And remarkably, Joshua's fear didn't stop him. I want that same kind of boldness because I don't feel very brave these days, especially with the huge pile of responsibility I carry. I don't feel equipped for it. I don't feel courageous enough to bear it. But I have no choice. So when I feel scared, remind me of Your promise to always be with me. Remind me that You're the One to supply me with everything I need. And help me embrace leadership with confidence, grateful for the opportunity to serve. In Jesus' name I pray, amen.

Since My servant Moses is now dead, you and the Israelites must prepare to cross over the Jordan River to enter the land I have given you.

JOSHUA 1:2 VOICE

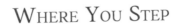

WHERE YOU STEP

Dear God, would I be more courageous if I knew without a doubt that everything would work out? If I knew my steps were always numbered and covered by Your favor, might I be more intrepid? If I knew I couldn't fail, would I be braver? Regardless, help me trust where You lead. Give me timely reminders that, no matter what, You're with me. You aren't looking for perfection. Instead, You're looking for a willing heart to follow You. Make my heart willing. Mature my faith. Show me how to walk audaciously. And make me gutsy enough to step out of my comfort zone as I choose to trust and follow You. In Jesus' name I pray, amen.

"I am giving you every place where you set foot, exactly as I promised Moses. . . . No one will be able to stand up against you during your lifetime. I will be with you in the same way I was with Moses. I won't desert you or leave you."
JOSHUA 1:3, 5 CEB

Maybe It's You

Dear God, it's hard to imagine that I may be part of the solution. I've never considered myself a leader because it felt too risky—too scary. For so long, I've sat back and let others take the lead. But I'm beginning to feel courage in my spirit. I'm starting to feel confident in my skills and abilities. Lord, if You're asking me to step into a leadership role, please make it crystal clear. Give me bravery to leave my comfort zone and engage in a new way. Provide me with clarity and vision for the next step. Put hope in my heart. I want to follow You and make a difference, so I say yes! In Jesus' name I pray, amen.

"Be brave and strong, because you are the one who will help this people take possession of the land, which I pledged to give to their ancestors."

Joshua 1:6 CEB

The Gift of Remembering

Dear God, I know the value of remembering promises You've spoken to me. It's in the scary moments when I want to quit that the importance of clinging to truth becomes clear. Thinking through all the ways You've shown up to save, heal, and restore in the past will be what bolsters my courage to stand strong in real time. Give me the mind to recall Your faithfulness when I need it the most. Fill my heart with the reality that You've always proved Yourself trustworthy. Keep the enemy from blocking my ability to recall hard proof of Your goodness in my life. I want to remember—I need to remember—because it strengthens me like nothing else can. In Jesus' name I pray, amen.

He said, "Remember what Moses the servant of GOD commanded you: GOD, your God, gives you rest and he gives you this land."
JOSHUA 1:13 MSG

When You Need New Friends

Dear God, I feel alone in my fear and pain. I'm walking through some difficult situations and I don't have good support to help me. I'm not sure when my community left, but they're not here now. Paul's courage increased when friends showed up, so bring new friends to me so my courage can increase too. I need encouragers to help me navigate, people who will have compassion and wisdom as I carefully walk this crooked path. And along with that, would You graciously give me the courage to let them in? Let me be appropriately vulnerable at the right times. Help me embrace their friendship. And help me be a good friend to them too. In Jesus' name I pray, amen.

And the [Christian] brethren there, having had news of us, came as far as the Forum of Appius and the Three Taverns to meet us. When Paul saw them, he thanked God and received new courage.

Acts 28:15 AMPC

WHEN YOU FEEL
BATTERED BY STONES

Dear God, when verbal stones are hurled at me, give me faith like Stephen. He didn't get offended and wish harm on those who hurt him. There weren't fights between him and the people pointing fingers. He didn't plot revenge. Instead, this great man of faith prayed. He went right to You, relying on his faith over any kind of fear or fury. What's more, Stephen forgave his persecutors. I want that for me. I want to be a modern-day Stephen, choosing to hold on to peace in the face of being battered by verbal stones. I can only do this through You. My only hope of keeping an eternal perspective is keeping my eyes on You, Lord! In Jesus' name I pray, amen.

As they battered him with stones, Stephen prayed, "Lord Jesus, accept my life!" Falling to his knees, he shouted, "Lord, don't hold this sin against them!" Then he died.
ACTS 7:59–60 CEB

FEAR MANIFESTING AS FINANCIAL OBSESSION

Dear God, I confess that my obsession with money stems from fear that I won't have enough in the future. I'm terrified of what might happen if I can't pay my bills. And rather than remember that You're always with me and will provide for my needs, I let myself get stirred up and stressed out. Bring the peace of Jesus to rest on my anxious heart. Show me the way to trust in You with my finances. Open my eyes to smart ways of budgeting and saving that I may be missing. And settle in my heart right now that You see me and love me and will never let me go. Today, I need to be reassured. In Jesus' name I pray, amen.

Don't be obsessed with money but live content with what you have, for you always have God's presence. For hasn't he promised you, "I will never leave you alone, never! And I will not loosen my grip on your life!"
HEBREWS 13:5 TPT

To Say It with Confidence

Dear God, there are many reasons I'm afraid right now, so let today's verse be my battle cry! From relationships to health to finances, I am lacking the kind of confidence mentioned in Hebrews. I want to anchor my hope in You, but it feels daunting to let go of the wheel. I'm used to being in control. And as much as I'd like to turn these fears over to You, I'm struggling to let go. Please grow my level of confidence in Your promises so I can find peace. Let me know deep in my DNA that You have my best interests at heart. I want to say with certainty that You're for me so I'm not afraid! In Jesus' name I pray, amen.

So we can say with great confidence:
"I know the Lord is for me and I will never
be afraid of what people may do to me!"
Hebrews 13:6 TPT

Not Caring What Others Think

Dear God, help me stop caring about what others think. I'm tired of giving it dominion over me. Why do I care what they think? All it does is hurt me, leaving me to feel ugly, unlovable, and unwanted. Why do I give others that kind of power over what I think about myself? Why do I fear their judgment? Lord, give me the boldness to focus only on what You think. When those insecurities pop up, let it drive me to Your Word, where I will find encouragement. It's where I'll discover who I am in You. And it will embolden me to live in freedom, trusting that my sense of value is nonnegotiable. In Jesus' name I pray, amen.

"Listen, my beloved friends, don't fear those who may want to take your life but can do nothing more. It's true that they may kill your body, but they have no power over your soul."
Luke 12:4 TPT

HE NEVER HIDES FROM YOU

Dear God, in those lonely moments, remind me that You aren't hiding from me. Sometimes I cry out and You feel so far away. I look for evidence of You working in my circumstance, but I can't see it. I crave to experience Your presence and peace, but it eludes me. And this is why I begin to lose hope. My fear multiplies in the loneliness, and I'm overwhelmed. There is nothing better than You to soothe an anxious heart. Only You can calm me when I'm scared and alone. Give me the eyes and ears to know You are always with me. You've promised never to leave or forsake me, and that powerful truth never fails. In Jesus' name I pray, amen.

*"You will look for Me intently,
and you will find Me."*
JEREMIAH 29:13 VOICE

GUTS AND GRIT

Dear God, I want the kind of guts and grit that Joseph of Arimathea showed when he asked Pilate for Jesus' body. I cannot imagine the fear that coursed through his veins as he mustered courage to approach the Roman governor. But he did, and I admire his valor! Let me dig deep and find that same level of nerve. With Your help, let me be bold as I advocate for myself and others. And let me be known as a fearless woman who stands firmly in her faith, an example to encourage the next generation to have courage. Not only is it freeing, but having unwavering confidence will allow me to make a difference in the world. In Jesus' name I pray, amen.

Late in the afternoon, since it was the Day of Preparation (that is, Sabbath eve), Joseph of Arimathea, a highly respected member of the Jewish Council, came. He was one who lived expectantly, on the lookout for the kingdom of God. Working up his courage, he went to Pilate and asked for Jesus' body.

MARK 15:42–43 MSG

MAKE ME BRAVE

Dear God, Esther was one gutsy girl. Knowing she could lose her life for exposing Haman's plan and asking the king to save her people didn't cause her to cower in fear. Instead, this queen's bravery sets a beautiful example for how I want to live. She was a risk taker. She put the needs of others before hers as she chose to stand up for a very worthy cause. She was relentless in pursing the calling on her life, even if it put her in peril. She was fearless. I don't feel strong right now, and I'm asking You to strengthen my faith so I can be a force to be reckoned with. Grow my confidence in You. Make me brave! In Jesus' name I pray, amen.

Queen Esther answered, "If I please the king, and if the king wishes, give me my life— that's my wish—and the lives of my people too. That's my desire. We have been sold—I and my people—to be wiped out, killed, and destroyed."
ESTHER 7:3–4 CEB

The Courage of Caleb

Dear God, so often I lack the confidence that Caleb showed. He saw the giants in the Promised Land, but they didn't deter him one bit because he knew You were involved. So rather than give in to fear or hopelessness, he trusted Your promises. I love that! I can think of many times when fear completely debilitated me. It knocked me down. It stole my joy and peace. But had I instead chosen to put my faith in You, I might have felt the same way Caleb did: resolved. I repent of the fear that's ruled my life. Forgive me. And from this day forward, fill me with courage and confidence to trust You no matter what. In Jesus' name I pray, amen.

Caleb interrupted, called for silence before Moses and said, "Let's go up and take the land—now. We can do it."
NUMBERS 13:30 MSG

FEAR CAN'T STOP YOU

Dear God, I don't ever want to stop serving You and my community. I want to be a light in this dark world, delivering joy and hope. But occasionally, I get a little timid. I feel insecure and wonder if I'm too much or not enough. I worry I'm annoying, and fear creeps in whispering lies that make me want to retreat. Give me courage to be unstoppable as I love the people You've placed in my life. Bless me with wisdom to know how I can serve them. Let me see the broken-hearted so I can pour compassion into their parched spirits. I don't want anything to keep me from being who You called me to be. In Jesus' name I pray, amen.

Do you suppose a few ruts in the road or rocks in the path are going to stop us? When the time comes, we'll be plenty ready to exchange exile for homecoming.

2 CORINTHIANS 5:8 MSG

EXPECTANT AND CONFIDENT

Dear God, I want to know without any doubt that You are working in my situation. I don't want to cross my fingers and hope. I don't want to waste my time wringing my hands in worry. I want to be full of confidence, assured that You're with me working out every mess I find myself in. I'm not alone! That's a gift You promised to every believer. And it gives me freedom to live with an expectant heart as well as informs how I approach every day. Let me be excited to see how You make a way. Let me be hopeful while I wait for it. And let me reject any fear that tries to take my joy away! In Jesus' name I pray, amen.

Look among the nations and watch!
Be astonished and stare because
something is happening in your days
that you wouldn't believe even if told.
HABAKKUK 1:5 CEB

POWERFUL ADVERTISING
FOR FAITH

Dear God, help me be humble so I recognize that I cannot navigate this life without You. Keep me from puffing up my chest with pride, boasting in my own strength and might as the reason I survived. The truth is I'm unable to thrive without You. I may be an educated and capable woman, but I am limited by the human condition. You are the One to calm the fears that beat me down. You suppress the insecurities telling me I'm not good enough. Your peace is what allows me to keep a healthy perspective in hard times. And when I am quick to give You the credit, it's powerful advertising for faith. In Jesus' name I pray, amen.

Yet we don't see ourselves as capable enough
to do anything in our own strength,
for our true competence flows from
God's empowering presence.

2 CORINTHIANS 3:5 TPT

CONFIDENCE BEFORE GOD

Dear God, sometimes I'm nervous to talk to You because I'm so aware of how wretched I can be. I'm afraid that You are disappointed in me or angry because of things I've done. I worry that I'm annoying when I ask for the same things over and over again. I'm concerned You may be frustrated because I still haven't figured it out. So the idea of being confident in prayer feels foreign. Please take that feeling from me. I don't want there to be anything that blocks my relationship with You. Instead, I want to believe without a doubt that my sins are forgiven and that Your love for me is unshakable. Help me replace any fear with steadfast faith. In Jesus' name I pray, amen.

And, beloved, if our consciences (our hearts) do not accuse us [if they do not make us feel guilty and condemn us], we have confidence (complete assurance and boldness) before God.
1 JOHN 3:21 AMPC

WISDOM FROM OTHERS

Dear God, help me find a community of people who are willing to share their stories with each other. It's such an encouragement to hear from others how they made it through a difficult situation. It helps grow my courage to know others survived stormy seasons of life. And it deepens my faith to hear them recount all the ways You intervened on their behalf. I need those truths to anchor me during my own storms. Too often, I've held on to my own ways of thinking. I've depended on my own strength, hoping it would help me power through. But no more. Open my heart to new friendships, and help me fearlessly embrace them. In Jesus' name I pray, amen.

If you think you know it all, you're
a fool for sure; real survivors
learn wisdom from others.
PROVERBS 28:26 MSG

THE KING OVER EVERYTHING

Dear God, help me keep my worldly support in perspective. I know You gave me amazing family and friends and use them in beautiful ways to walk me through tough times. But I also know that You are my source, plain and simple. Your name is above all names. And when I'm battling fear and worry and anxiety, my first stop should be prayer. Give me a healthy view of my community and the role each person is to play in my life, and help me keep my eyes on You first and foremost. They are my earthly warriors full of might, but You are the King over everything! Let me never invert the two. In Jesus' name I pray, amen.

See those people polishing their chariots,
and those others grooming their horses?
But we're making garlands for GOD our God.
The chariots will rust, those horses pull up
lame—and we'll be on our feet, standing tall.
PSALM 20:7–8 MSG

THANK YOU!

Dear God, too often I forget to thank You for all You've done. Let me remedy that right now. I've been delivered from debilitating fear in places I never thought possible. I have found victory from anxiety over certain issues that have plagued me for years. I'm more confident now than I've ever been, and I'm certain of Your hand in that. I'm learning to be bold as I advocate for my needs and speak up for others struggling to say what's on their mind. I feel strong in my resolve to trust You as we battle the giants in front of me. And I owe every bit of this to Your promise of faithfulness. Thank You! In Jesus' name I pray, amen.

May Yahweh give you every desire of your heart and carry out your every plan as you go to battle. When you succeed, we will celebrate and shout for joy. Flags will fly when victory is yours! Yes, God will answer your prayers and we will praise him!

PSALM 20:4–5 TPT

UNSTOPPABLE

Dear God, sometimes I end up in a negative mindset. Whether I'm overwhelmed by the mess I'm in or I'm starting to fear what I'm facing, my attitude plummets. It hits rock bottom. But I realize it's because I've taken my eyes off You. I've stopped trusting that You see exactly what's happening and are already in the mix, working things out for my benefit and Your glory. So that I'm not a Negative Nelly, refresh my heart to have faith in You. My enemy will not prevail when I choose to believe Your promises to save and protect. In Your name, I can rise up in courage and face fierce enemies with confidence. With You, I'm unstoppable. In Jesus' name I pray, amen.

Our enemies will not prevail; they will only collapse and perish in defeat while we will rise up, full of courage.
PSALM 20:8 TPT

Courage to Embrace Today

Dear God, give me courage to embrace whatever today brings. Remove any fear that keeps me from being present with those I love. Help me focus on the good things happening right now so I don't wander down the path of despair. I'm not able to predict the future, so I need to stop trying. Instead, fill me with peace in knowing that You see what's coming and are already working things out for my benefit and Your glory. Mature my faith so I can relax as I trust You with anything the future holds. I may not know what comes next, but I know the One who does. He loves me without fail, and that's enough for me. In Jesus' name I pray, amen.

The reality is you have no idea where your life will take you tomorrow. You are like a mist that appears one moment and then vanishes another.

James 4:14 voice

GIVING GOD YOUR TOMORROWS

Dear God, I can't sit in the fear of tomorrow any longer. It keeps me up at night, robbing me of much-needed sleep. It steals my joy throughout the day as the stress creeps in unexpectedly. It makes me project terrible outcomes down the road that leave me feeling completely hopeless. For my heart's sake, I need to leave these fears and anxieties at Your feet and trust You to handle every one of them. I'm just so overwhelmed with dread for what the future may hold and tired of fighting the onslaught of negatives. Give me the strength to let go of control and let You take the wheel. You are the better driver anyway. In Jesus' name I pray, amen.

Instead you should say, "Our tomorrows are in the Lord's hands and if he is willing we will live life to its fullest and do this or that."

JAMES 4:15 TPT

145

THE COURAGE TO HELP OTHERS GROW

Dear God, if I'm here to help other believers grow their faith, I need help, because I don't feel like a leader myself. I don't feel responsible enough to influence others. Sometimes I battle debilitating fear as I step out of my comfort zone and trust You when life falls apart. I worry that You're too busy for my issues. And while I know I should be clinging to You for hope, too often I sit in my stress and strife alone. So how can I be a spiritual leader? Help me trust that if You call me to this, it means You will also equip me to walk it out. And make me fearless as I do. In Jesus' name I pray, amen.

Now, those who are mature in their faith can easily be recognized, for they don't live to please themselves but have learned to patiently embrace others in their immaturity. Our goal must be to empower others to do what is right and good for them, and to bring them into spiritual maturity.

ROMANS 15:1–2 TPT

THE FEAR OF UNITY

Dear God, help me be a team player and willing to embrace community. I'm so used to flying solo because it just feels safer. I struggle trusting others, terrified they won't do what they promised. I'm afraid to let anyone know the real me because I feel so unworthy and unacceptable. I don't want to place my faith in people who I know will eventually fail me. So instead of helping create unity, I hide. Make me brave so I can venture out and open my heart to new friendships. Give me grace to realize no one is perfect, so I shouldn't expect them to be. And give me confidence to know I am wonderfully made on purpose! In Jesus' name I pray, amen.

Now may God, the source of great endurance and comfort, grace you with unity among yourselves, which flows from your relationship with Jesus, the Anointed One.

ROMANS 15:5 TPT

OVERCOMING INTIMIDATION

Dear God, give me a heart for others, especially those who make me feel inferior. Help me love and celebrate them rather than quietly hope they fail. Sometimes I sit in judgment of someone because she intimidates me. Looking at her life makes me feel insecure about mine. And I'm afraid to be myself since my life lacks the zest hers does—at least in my opinion. You made each of us special. We are made on purpose. Let me see everyone in this light. Give me courage to consider everyone valuable, each in their own way. And please help me love who I am and how You made me. I'm tired of the anxiety that comes with craving acceptance. In Jesus' name I pray, amen.

So accept one another in the same
way the Anointed has accepted you so
that God will get the praise He is due.
ROMANS 15:7 VOICE

ASKING OTHERS TO PRAY

Dear God, I get so nervous asking others to pray for me. I wish I had the confidence of Paul in today's verse when he boldly asked for help. He didn't show any timidity at all! I end up worried that my requests will be ignored. I worry that someone might think they are silly or trivial. What if I ask for prayer in confidence and then they share it with someone else? It just feels too risky, like a setup to be embarrassed. Lord, You're going to have to bring my heart around on this one. You'll need to make me courageous enough to be vulnerable with others. And I am asking that You do! In Jesus' name I pray, amen.

Brothers and sisters, I urge you, through our Lord Jesus Christ and through the love of the Spirit, to join me in my struggles in your prayers to God for me.

ROMANS 15:30 CEB

Trusting His Plan

Dear God, I realize I don't need to stress out about what comes next. I get to dream and hope all I want, trusting that You know the desire of my heart and that it will come to pass if it's Your will. This knowledge takes pressure off me to perform. I don't have to wring my hands, hoping I can make some headway with my dreams. Before I was born, You numbered my days. You know every step I'll take before I see You face-to-face. So I choose not to be afraid of missing out or messing up. Instead, I'll make beautiful plans and trust You'll bring them to fruition if it's Your perfect will. In Jesus' name I pray, amen.

It would be best to say, "If it is the Lord's will and we live long enough, we hope to do this project or pursue that dream."
James 4:15 voice

No Reason to Fear

Dear God, I need You. I'm not feeling confident in what I'm facing. I lack the strength of mind and spirit to stand strong. And too often, I either cower in fear or try to handle everything myself. I know this isn't Your plan. You never intended for me to stand alone in my pain and anxiety. Give me the kind of faith that allows me to rise up and use my voice. There is no good reason to live in discouragement and despair. Life may be hard, but with You it can be beautiful too. I get to choose if people and situations bring me down. I get to choose if I isolate. Give me the courage to stand strong instead. In Jesus' name I pray, amen.

*So why should I fear in bad times, hemmed in
by enemy malice, shoved around by bullies,
demeaned by the arrogant rich? Really!
There's no such thing as self-rescue,
pulling yourself up by your bootstraps.*
PSALM 49:5–7 MSG

DON'T BE IMPRESSED

Dear God, keep me from being jealous of those who have more than me. Even though it's hard to watch them live what I consider an easy life, I have no idea what's happening behind closed doors. They may be miserable in their marriage, have unhealed pain, struggle with addictions, or completely hate their life. I need to focus on being the best me and living in gratitude for what I've been given. At the root of my envious feelings is fear that I'm not as good as they are. I worry I'll never measure up. But the truth is I'm not supposed to find my worth by comparing myself to others. Remind me I'm valuable simply because I'm Yours. In Jesus' name I pray, amen.

So don't be impressed with those who get rich and pile up fame and fortune. They can't take it with them; fame and fortune all get left behind.
PSALM 49:16–17 MSG

COURAGE FOR THE HARD THINGS

Dear God, help me be effective for what's ahead. I already feel the struggle, for the battle will most certainly be uphill. I have amazing support from friends and family, but I need You most of all. I am scared because there's much at stake and I don't want to make the wrong choices. I know that when I feel weak, You will make me strong. When I'm confused, You will bring wisdom. In those times when I'm overrun with worry, I can always find peace through You. Today, I am asking for all of those things. Thank You for being a hands-on God who promises never to leave us alone to figure things out. In Jesus' name I pray, amen.

Give us help for the hard task; human help is worthless. In God we'll do our very best; he'll flatten the opposition for good.

PSALM 60:11–12 MSG

FEAR OF TAKING THE WRONG PATH

Dear God, I'm so confused about my next step. All signs seem to point in this one direction, but there is a check in my spirit, and I don't know if it's You or not. I'm anxious about doing the wrong thing because I don't want to step out of Your will for me. For most of my life I've been a wreck, not concerned about who I hurt or disappointed. I lived for myself and did what made me happy. But now that I am following You, I care. I want to walk the narrow path of faith so my words and actions point others to You. I want to do the right thing. Help me know what it is. In Jesus' name I pray, amen.

*Before every person there is a path
that seems like the right one to take,
but it leads straight to hell!*
PROVERBS 16:25 TPT

MONEY DOESN'T SAVE

Dear God, keep me from thinking money is my savior. Hoarding it won't save me from pain or heartache. Working myself into the ground won't protect me from the things that scare me. Obsessing about how much I have will not shelter me from battling insecurity. There's nothing on earth that can fill the role of You, Lord. You alone are my Strong Tower and Shield. Help me keep my eyes fixed on that truth so I don't put my trust in anyone or anything else to meet my needs and defend my heart. Help me have a healthy appreciation of money, remembering I can't take it with me as I spend eternity with You. In Jesus' name I pray, amen.

The rich think their wealth protects them;
they imagine themselves safe behind it.
PROVERBS 18:11 MSG

A Healthy Fear of Pride

Dear God, keep me humble. Give me a heart willing to consider the ideas of others, knowing my ways aren't always best. I know You dislike pride, so please mature in me the ability to have a healthy fear of it. I don't want anything to cause issues between us. Make me someone who creates a safe place to share ideas. Let me be one to encourage collaboration. Let me be willing to listen to advice as well as give it when asked. And let me be open to what others say, honoring their willingness to be vulnerable and honest with their opinions. But mostly, let my ears be trained to hear Your voice through it all. In Jesus' name I pray, amen.

There's only one thing worse than a fool,
and that's the smug, conceited man always
in love with his own opinions.
Proverbs 26:12 TPT

DISCERNMENT FOR TRUTH

Dear God, give me discernment to see the truth. Sometimes it's easy to follow the rabbit trail of conspiracy theories because it gives me space to ruminate about situations, trying to connect dots. It can remove the blame from me and put it other places or on other people. But it also has a way of destabilizing me and conjuring up fear. I don't need my thoughts running a million miles in the wrong direction. Instead, I need a clear mind to find the truth. I need to trust You to clear the fog of confusion. And I don't want to sit in unnecessary fear over something that's baseless. I know that's not Your will for me. In Jesus' name I pray, amen.

"Don't be like this people, always afraid somebody is plotting against them. Don't fear what they fear. Don't take on their worries."
ISAIAH 8:12 MSG

Cling to God

Dear God, help me guard my eyes so that all I see is truth. There is so much deception in the world today, and I don't want to get caught up in it any longer. I don't want to be easily tricked or misled. In Your goodness, please give me wisdom to know what I'm dealing with and discernment to choose the right path. Keep me from being so set in my ways that I'm unable to consider something different. Don't allow fear to keep me stuck in the wrong narrative. I only want Your truth to rule in my life. I want You to be my north star. And the only thing I want to cling to is You. In Jesus' name I pray, amen.

"But instead, you are clinging to lies and illusions that are worthless."
JEREMIAH 7:8 VOICE

FEARING WEAKNESSES

Dear God, it seems wrong to feel good about my weaknesses. Usually, I work very hard to hide them from others. In all honesty, I'm often worried that I'll be judged or criticized because of them. I'm afraid of looking powerless or frail. So to feel better about myself, I do everything I can to present an all-together version of me. But You don't want that. I love knowing You don't see my flaws and limitations as a negative. To You, they are just an opportunity to shine Your glory through them. So Lord, please give me bold confidence in my imperfectness. Keep me from fearing what others may think. And let me find my strength in You! In Jesus' name I pray, amen.

If boasting is necessary, I will boast about examples of my weakness.
2 CORINTHIANS 11:30 TPT

HE IS THE FIRM FOUNDATION

Dear God, I don't have to be afraid because You are my firm Foundation. If I can keep this perspective when the storms of life hit and I get scared, I'll be able to find footing in my faith. At the end of the day, You're all I have anyway. You are the constant—the One who never changes. So when my world feels chaotic and confusing, I can always cling to You to steady me. There is no fear too big, no problem too complex, no worry too weighty, and no insecurity too tangled for You. Help me remember to turn to You first. And be quick to catch me when I fall. In Jesus' name I pray, amen.

*The fundamental fact of existence is
that this trust in God, this faith, is the firm
foundation under everything that makes
life worth living. It's our handle on what we
can't see. The act of faith is what distinguished
our ancestors, set them above the crowd.*
HEBREWS 11:1–2 MSG

Ask God to Meet You

Dear God, meet me in my fear and bring it under Your control. I'm paralyzed in it and feel hopeless. I can't find my footing to get up and catch my breath, and I'm worried. I've made a mess of my life, and I'm unable to clean it up. I desperately need You right now. I'm choosing to trust that I'll find peace through Jesus, so I'm taking You up on Your offer of always being available. Please come quickly to stop my anxiety. Cover me in calm. Remind me of Your love. Show me that I matter. And speak encouragement into my spirit. Meet me more than halfway and free me from this debilitating fear. I need You. In Jesus' name I pray, amen.

God met me more than halfway,
he freed me from my anxious fears.
Psalm 34:4 msg

DESPERATE AND DEFEATED

Dear God, I'm hurting. It feels like so much is going wrong in my life, and I'm worried that things won't get better. It's been a long road—so many years of continued heartbreak—and I'm losing stamina. I've tried being brave, but it didn't last long. I've tried standing up for myself, but I lacked real courage to maintain it. In the end, I'm still here, stuck. Hear my voice and wrap me in Your arms. Don't leave me to figure this out alone. Help me feel safe and secure. I'm feeble and in need of Your deliverance. I'm at the end of me and surrendering every fear to You. Please save me and restore my broken heart. In Jesus' name I pray, amen.

When I had nothing, desperate and defeated, I cried out to the Lord and he heard me, bringing his miracle-deliverance when I needed it most.

PSALM 34:6 TPT

GOD IS SO GOOD!

Dear God, You are so good! I stepped out in faith and trusted You with my fears, and I'm now blessed with peace. I chose to surrender my insecurities, and You grew my confidence. When I admitted my anxiety, it was supernaturally replaced with fearlessness to move forward. How wonderful that You are who You say You are! And how powerful to watch You do what You say You'll do! I am so grateful for Your faithfulness to make good on promises from the Word. What an encouragement to my weary soul to see things in my life shift in such meaningful ways. Thank You for being able and willing to deliver me from bondage. In Jesus' name I pray, amen.

Taste of His goodness; see how wonderful the Eternal truly is. Anyone who puts trust in Him will be blessed and comforted.

PSALM 34:8 VOICE

THE COURAGE TO WALK AWAY

Dear God, how can I seek peace when I'm so tangled up in fear? Evil has plagued me for so long. Fear and I have a long history together. It's something the women in my family have passed down for generations. It's discussions we have every time we talk. I worry all the time and about everything. Help me release that fear as I choose faith instead. Help me speak out Your truth until it becomes my truth too. I want to live and love well, empowered to speak encouragement. I know with Your help I can retrain my mind to respond differently and I can walk away from the fear that has held me for so long. In Jesus' name I pray, amen.

If you love life and want to live a good, long time, take care with the things you say. Don't lie or spread gossip or talk about improper things. Walk away from the evil things of the world, and always seek peace and pursue it.

PSALM 34:12–14 VOICE

In Need of Deliverance

Dear God, I cannot believe this is my life. How did I get here, and will I ever be happy again? Will I ever not be triggered by fear? Will I find deliverance from this chaos? I need You right now, Lord. Bring me out of this dark valley and back into the wide-open spaces full of sunshine. Bless me with courage and confidence to fight on so I don't run away again, scared and hopeless. I want to be healed from this pattern of living. I want to see a new season of life full of freedom. I want to taste and see Your goodness and be encouraged. Hear my cries from this pit and come quickly! In Jesus' name I pray, amen.

When the righteous cry out, the LORD listens; he delivers them from all their troubles. The LORD is close to the brokenhearted; he saves those whose spirits are crushed.

PSALM 34:17–18 CEB

TRYING TO IMPRESS OTHERS

Dear God, I know that being afraid of people will only get me in trouble. Unfortunately, I know this firsthand. In the past, fear has made me do things I wouldn't normally do. It's caused me loads of stress as I worked endlessly to try to impress someone. It's encouraged me to compromise who I am in hopes of getting their seal of approval. And worst of all, it's made them my god, putting them above You. Forgive me. If I want my life to glorify You, then I need to change how I'm living. My trust needs to be firmly anchored in You alone. Starting today, I'm choosing to put You first. Let my life reveal this decision! In Jesus' name I pray, amen.

The fear of man brings a snare, but whoever leans on, trusts in, and puts his confidence in the Lord is safe and set on high.

PROVERBS 29:25 AMPC

LEARNING TO DUCK

Dear God, bless me with the wisdom to see trouble coming my way so I can duck. I'm asking for spiritual eyes so I can perceive the situation clearly and avoid being caught off guard all the time. So often, I feel exposed and afraid, unprotected in a world where evil is prevalent. Sure, there will be some situations that blow in without warning, but if I am wise and watchful, I'll be able to prepare myself for what's coming. I may not have the ability to prevent it, but I can prepare my heart. Help me live unafraid of the future. By trusting in You, I can have confidence that things will work out. In Jesus' name I pray, amen.

A prudent person sees trouble coming and ducks; a simpleton walks in blindly and is clobbered.
PROVERBS 27:12 MSG

Courageously Joyful

Dear God, give me the courage to be a joyful woman. Even when my life is a mess and I'm feeling overwhelmed, allow me to find the silver lining in my circumstances. Let me focus on the good rather than give in to the weight of the struggle. Living this way will point others to You, especially when they realize You're the reason for my hope. I don't want to be a fearful person. I don't want bad news to rule my heart. Instead, let the words I say and the things I do reveal my steadfast faith. Whether I'm struggling in a relationship, afraid financially, or worried about my kids, help me be courageously joyful as I trust You. In Jesus' name I pray, amen.

Let this hope burst forth within you, releasing a continual joy. Don't give up in a time of trouble, but commune with God at all times.

Romans 12:12 TPT

It's a Gift?

Dear God, it's challenging for me to see hard seasons as a gift. It feels counterintuitive, considering how I feel most of the time. When I'm sitting in fear and insecurity, being joyful isn't usually my first response. Too often, I give in to the negative thoughts. I let the feelings of hopelessness win. Lord, I need Your strength to keep me engaged in the battle. I need confidence to stay in the moment rather than look for an escape route. I need bold faith to believe You are in the details. Help me trust that You allowed this fearful season only because it will help grow my faith. And give me the courage to stand. In Jesus' name I pray, amen.

Consider it a sheer gift, friends, when tests
and challenges come at you from all sides.
You know that under pressure, your faith-life is
forced into the open and shows its true colors.
So don't try to get out of anything prematurely.
Let it do its work so you become mature and
well-developed, not deficient in any way.

James 1:2–4 msg

EMPOWERED BY CONFIDENT FAITH

Dear God, I need wisdom to know the next right step in this situation. In my pride, I always think I know best. But in my fear, the truth is I'm terrified to make a mistake. The enemy is so quick to whisper reminders of all the times I tried and failed. Too often, I listen. And honestly, asking for help feels like weakness because as a grown woman I should know the answers, right? Humble me, Lord. Teach me to surrender my ways to Yours. Give me the right perspective so I see clearly. Give me courage to advocate for myself as I ask for help. And empower me to live in freedom through confident faith. In Jesus' name I pray, amen.

And if anyone longs to be wise, ask God for wisdom and he will give it! He won't see your lack of wisdom as an opportunity to scold you over your failures but he will overwhelm your failures with his generous grace. Just make sure you ask empowered by confident faith without doubting that you will receive.

JAMES 1:5–6 TPT

FEAR OF NOT PASSING THE TEST

Dear God, Your Word says that having bold faith in hard times will bring about blessings. What's more, it says I will find true happiness when I trust You through them. This is something I can only do with Your help because I'm simply not strong enough to weather the storms I'm facing alone. I don't have Your ability to see the ins and outs of the situation. I'm worried about how it will all work out in the end. . .and panicked that it may not. So I'm pressing into You today, Lord, asking for an increase of faith. Teach me to trust You for the courage and confidence I need to pass every test. In Jesus' name I pray, amen.

If your faith remains strong, even while surrounded by life's difficulties, you will continue to experience the untold blessings of God! True happiness comes as you pass the test with faith, and receive the victorious crown of life promised to every lover of God!

JAMES 1:12 TPT

WHEN FEAR MANIFESTS
AS ANGER

Dear God, I confess my struggle with anger. It seems to pop up so easily these days, often without any warning. And I know that underneath the anger is fear. I'm learning that when something makes me scared, it often manifests as frustration or rage. But I don't want to be known for my anger or my fear. Instead, I want to leave a legacy of grace. I want to be a joy carrier. I hope others feel loved and valued by me more than anything else. Because anger robs others of seeing those things in me, give me confidence to trust You in all things. And when anger or fear arises, fill me with a sense of Your peace. In Jesus' name I pray, amen.

Listen, open your ears, harness your desire to speak, and don't get worked up into a rage so easily, my brothers and sisters. Human anger is a futile exercise that will never produce God's kind of justice in this world.

JAMES 1:19–20 VOICE

Fear of Saying
the Wrong Thing

Dear God, help me be mindful of the words I use with others. Let me be an encourager, especially because there seems to be so few of them in the world these days. When hard things need to be shared, help me be someone who offers the truth with love sprinkled in. I want to be sure my words are measured rather than reckless. I want them to be intentional and thoughtful. But in this pursuit, don't let me become so fearful of saying the wrong things that I keep silent. I don't want to be timid or shy. Instead, give me the wisdom and courage to speak at the right time and in the right way. In Jesus' name I pray, amen.

If those who claim devotion to God
don't control what they say, they mislead
themselves. Their devotion is worthless.
JAMES 1:26 CEB

BOLD ENOUGH TO ASK

Dear God, I confess that I'm scared to ask You for certain things. Not all things, just some. The reason is that they feel trivial or unimportant. In the grand scheme of things, these requests seem silly. They feel either too big or too out there. And I don't want to bog You down with ask after ask. Help me remember I don't exhaust You. Remind me You want to hear what's on my heart. And make me brave enough to put any request before You with confidence. Even more, help me trust that however and whenever You choose to answer me is always for my benefit and Your glory, so I can be grateful no matter what. In Jesus' name I pray, amen.

"Until now you've not been bold enough to ask the Father for a single thing in my name, but now you can ask, and keep on asking him! And you can be sure that you'll receive what you ask for, and your joy will have no limits!"

JOHN 16:24 TPT

A BEAUTIFUL LIFE

Dear God, I want everything You planned for my life. I'm full of hope and energy, ready to live out my days with purpose and passion. My heart is full of determination to have my life reflect Your goodness. But sometimes fear gets in the way. I worry I might make a wrong choice or run out of steam. What if I let others down? More importantly, what if I let You down? Help me take a step back so I don't run ahead of You, and give me the spiritual eyes and ears to follow Your lead. I know that with my willingness and Your favor, I can live a beautiful life that makes a difference. In Jesus' name I pray, amen.

Instead, You direct me on the path that leads to a beautiful life. As I walk with You, the pleasures are never-ending, and I know true joy and contentment.

PSALM 16:11 VOICE

CELEBRATING GOD

Dear God, forgive me for all the times I've doubted You. Too often, I've found myself worrying that You aren't going to show up in my stressful situation. I've told myself You're too busy with bigger issues to listen to mine. I've wondered if You get tired of hearing the same frustrations and fears from me over and over again. And without my wanting it to, that mindset ends up shutting me down and shutting me up. I'm sorry for letting anxiety and insecurity come between us. Help cultivate in me a heart of joy and gladness. Let me enjoy our relationship! Open my eyes to the ways You're working in my life and let's celebrate Your kindness and faithfulness! In Jesus' name I pray, amen.

This is the very day GOD acted—
let's celebrate and be festive!
PSALM 118:24 MSG

WORRIED FOR JOY

Dear God, sometimes I worry that I'll never find joy again. This season of life has been so difficult that I'm fearful happiness will always elude me. There doesn't seem to be anything worth hoping for, especially because my heart can't handle being let down again. I'm struggling to find my happy place right now. So I'm thankful for the reminder that You are the Joy Giver. No matter what the world may offer as a short-term solution, You promise to fill me with lasting joy even in the toughest times. It's through Your goodness that I can be fulfilled, feeling whole in heart again. You're the One who will make joy overflow into the good times and the tough seasons. In Jesus' name I pray, amen.

The intense pleasure you give me surpasses the gladness of harvest time, even more than when the harvesters gaze upon their ripened grain and when their new wine overflows.

PSALM 4:7 TPT

HIS ARMS ARE
ALWAYS OPEN

Dear God, when I really mess up, I worry about being rejected by those that matter to me. I start obsessing about what they will think of my bad choices. I worry about being judged and criticized in hurtful ways. It scares me. But in Your steadfast love for me, I'm always welcomed with open arms. Thank You for not holding my imperfections against me. I appreciate that Your heart for me is always good and not dependent on me being flawless. And I'm so grateful that my wrong decisions and weak choices don't scare You away and that I can't sin enough to turn You off. That in and of itself is worthy of celebration! In Jesus' name I pray, amen.

But you'll welcome us with open arms when we run for cover to you. Let the party last all night! Stand guard over our celebration. You are famous, GOD, for welcoming God-seekers, for decking us out in delight.
PSALM 5:11–12 MSG

THE COURAGE TO BE
A GOOD FRIEND

Dear God, give me the courage to be present with my family and friends regardless of what they are going through. When they have something to celebrate, let me join in with fervor. Give me the energy to recognize their victory or accomplishment, always making time for them! On the flip side, when they are struggling, let my heart be full of compassion. Help me meet them in their pain and grief in meaningful ways, showing them the care they need in that moment. Don't let me back away because I don't know how to respond. Keep me from finding convenient excuses. Instead, make me confident enough to meet every need they have. In Jesus' name I pray, amen.

Laugh with your happy friends when they're happy; share tears when they're down.
ROMANS 12:15 MSG

THE GOD WHO COMFORTS

Dear God, I love that You are such a calming force in my life. When my relationships feel chaotic, You are quick to bring my heart into alignment. You're the One to shift expectations when I begin to worry. When the bad news sucker punches me in the gut, it's Your kindness that lets me find rest. You make things feel manageable when stress tries to stir up my emotions. Your love calms my anxieties when they begin to flare. And when peace feels distant, all I have to do is ask for Your help. Thank You for knowing the value and importance of bringing comfort. I'm so blessed by the reassurance You so generously give. In Jesus' name I pray, amen.

When my anxieties multiply,
your comforting calms me down.
PSALM 94:19 CEB

HE IS THE CHAMPION

Dear God, please rescue me. Be my Champion. Give me hope that I can overcome the debilitating fear that plagues me. I'm worried about many things right now—things that matter greatly to me. I have anxiety about how everything will work out. I'm concerned that I'll be stuck in this place forever. I've tried so many things to lessen the stress, but I can't seem to find the relief I need. Lord, please intervene. I want to feel Your goodness and delight. Let me hear Your voice over all the others. Bring a sense of peace to my fears so they melt away. But most of all, please fill my heart with joy in knowing You're with me. In Jesus' name I pray, amen.

The Eternal your God is standing right here among you, and He is the champion who will rescue you. He will joyfully celebrate over you; He will rest in His love for you; He will joyfully sing because of you like a new husband.

ZEPHANIAH 3:17 VOICE

A POWERFUL
RESPONSE TO FEAR

Dear God, help me courageously stand for truth in a world that feels so dark. Let me be a light that shines brightly for You. Bring opportunities my way so I can share my powerful testimony of Your goodness. Every time I feel fear start to rise in me, my response will be to speak even louder. When stress starts to build, I will bless more people in Your name. When I'm feeling worried, I will proclaim Your glory even louder. I am choosing to fully trust that You will strengthen me in every battle and shield me from every danger. And every time I see You move in mighty ways, I will rejoice and give You all the praise! In Jesus' name I pray, amen.

Yahweh is my strength and my wraparound shield from. When I fully trust in you, help is on the way. I jump for joy and burst forth with ecstatic, passionate praise! I will sing songs of what you mean to me!

PSALM 28:7 TPT

THE GOD WHO SHOWS UP

Dear God, sometimes I need a reminder that since You showed up for me before, You will do it again. That's not a hope; it's a promise You've made that means so much to me. In hard times, it's important that I think back over all the ways You made something wrong very right. It's powerful when I'm able to remember situations where You rescued me from the enemy's traps. Lord, please bless me with a supernatural memory to recall Your power and mercy in my life. Let the memories strengthen my belief. Let them mature my faith. And use them to encourage me to be patient as I wait for Your hand to move in the difficult times. In Jesus' name I pray, amen.

And now, GOD, do it again—bring rains to our drought-stricken lives so those who planted their crops in despair will shout "Yes!" at the harvest, so those who went off with heavy hearts will come home laughing, with armloads of blessing.

PSALM 126:4–6 MSG

THE FEAR OF MEETING IN PERSON

Dear God, I know the value of community. I know You designed it for our benefit. Being with those we care about and who care about us has powerful benefits. It helps as we work through issues, encouraging us along the way. It reminds us we are loved and necessary. But living in this digital age has kept us from thriving in the personal connections we were made to crave. And for me, it's created fear and anxiety to meet with my friends and family face-to-face. I know they care, but I'm scared to be vulnerable in person. It feels too exposing. Change my heart, Lord. Help me overcome fear and insecurity. Help me trust those who love me. In Jesus' name I pray, amen.

I have a lot more things to tell you, but I'd rather not use paper and ink. I hope to be there soon in person and have a heart-to-heart talk. That will be far more satisfying to both you and me. Everyone here in your sister congregation sends greetings.
2 John 1:12–13 MSG

WORRIED IT WON'T GET BETTER?

Dear God, what if nothing in my situation changes? What if nothing improves and I am stuck in these impossible places for the rest of my life? Deep down, I'm afraid this may be the best my life gets, and it leaves me feeling terribly hopeless. But I believe You have better plans for me! You promise to bring joy to replace the fearful and insecure feelings. You infuse hope every time I need it. Lord, You offer peace for my anxious heart in the middle of my mourning. Remind me to cry out for Your help every time I'm feeling overwhelmed and worried. In Your great love there's a promise of saving and restoring that is unmatched! In Jesus' name I pray, amen.

You changed my mourning into dancing. You took off my funeral clothes and dressed me up in joy.
PSALM 30:11 CEB

HE IS ON THE JOB

Dear God, forgive me for all the times I've questioned where You were in my situation. I'm sorry that my default response has been to think You've abandoned me. The Word is crystal clear that I am never alone, because Your glorious presence is steadfast and constant. You never walk away from me, be it good or tough times. So rather than let fear take root, may I be strong. Help me understand the privilege of hard seasons as they work to mature my faith. Even more, remind me it's an honor to experience some of what Jesus did while on earth. I'm resolved not to become afraid when my circumstances get messy because I know You are on the job. In Jesus' name I pray, amen.

Friends, when life gets really difficult, don't jump to the conclusion that God isn't on the job. Instead, be glad that you are in the very thick of what Christ experienced. This is a spiritual refining process, with glory just around the corner.

1 PETER 4:12–13 MSG

REJOICE INSTEAD

Dear God, every time I'm struggling with fear or frustration, I will choose to give You praise. Rather than sit in those unproductive feelings and feel worried for another second, I am going to lift up my voice and rejoice that You are good! The truth is I'm tired of feeling defeated. It's exhausting to always be in an emotional crisis and anxious about the outcome. So from today forward, I will focus solely on Your promises to save and will believe that You're already at work in my stressful situation. I'm not a helpless victim. Because of You, I am not a weak or inferior woman. And starting right now, my loud faith will make sure everyone knows it. In Jesus' name I pray, amen.

Lift up a great shout of joy to Yahweh!
Go ahead and do it—everyone, everywhere!
PSALM 100:1 TPT

How Praying and Celebrating Helps

Dear God, whether in fearful times or courageous moments, I will put a priority on growing my relationship with You. I'm fully aware of how desperately I need Your courage, wisdom, and strength in my life every day. I need Your gentle guidance for the next steps as I try to navigate the curveballs that come my way. Thank You for helping me—even if I'm still struggling with a bit of fear. Thank You for the freedom to place my requests before You. I simply cannot walk through life without You! Help me be joyous no matter what. Encourage my heart to celebrate Your goodness and faithfulness. And let my testimony always point to You. In Jesus' name I pray, amen.

Celebrate always, pray constantly,
and give thanks to God no matter
what circumstances you find yourself in.
1 Thessalonians 5:16–18 voice

WISDOM WINS

Dear God, when I am battling any type of fear, let me be quick to ask You for wisdom. Sometimes I get lost in thoughts that lead me down the rabbit hole of anxiety. In those moments, what I need more than anything are clear thoughts so I can discern truth from lies. I need Your help to cut through the confusion. And because I'm so limited by my humanity, most situations require the kind of wisdom only You can provide. I don't have to fear anything because You are with me. But when I get confused and forget that beautiful truth, please bless me with clear eyes to see the path You've uncovered before me. In Jesus' name I pray, amen.

You're blessed when you meet Lady Wisdom,
when you make friends with Madame Insight.
She's worth far more than money in the bank;
her friendship is better than a big salary.
PROVERBS 3:13–14 MSG

THE TENSION BETWEEN CAREFUL AND FEARFUL

Dear God, help me be careful how I live, but not fearful. There's an interesting tension between the two. Too often, my pursuit of mindful living has ended up giving me all sorts of anxiety. I became scared of messing up or letting others down. I tried to make wise choices but then beat myself up when I chose wrong. My desire is always to live a good and faithful life with You. I want my words and actions to honor Your name. I want my life to shine a spotlight on faithful living and bring others into a saving relationship with You. Please don't let fear keep me from that. Instead, would You help me have a healthy perspective? In Jesus' name I pray, amen.

So be very careful how you live, not being like those with no understanding, but live honorably with true wisdom, for we are living in evil times. Take full advantage of every day as you spend your life for his purposes.
EPHESIANS 5:15–16 TPT

Unafraid to Listen and Learn

Dear God, give me courage to listen to the advice of others. Let me have an open heart and mind to those who care for me and want the best. It's hard to hear truth sometimes, and there's often shame attached to receiving it. But I know if I can humble myself and trust You, what's shared could be life giving. So please give me a willing heart to learn from the wisdom of others. Let me be open to accepting their words. And surround me with people who care enough to be honest and encouraging. In the end, let me be remembered as one unafraid to listen and learn—and for how that act of humility made my life sweeter. In Jesus' name I pray, amen.

Listen well to wise counsel and be willing to learn from correction so that by the end of your life you'll be known for your wisdom.
PROVERBS 19:20 TPT

Fear of Being Teachable

Dear God, I'm going to be brutally honest with You. This one is hard to admit because it feels ugly. It's prideful. But it's truth. I know the way to heal is to reveal, and that's why I'm sharing this with You right now. So here goes. . . I am in love with my own opinions. I think I make the right choices, most of the time. I think I am smart and mindful, which will give me a heads-up when decisions need to be made. And it scares me to let anyone else be in charge. I'm not teachable because I always want to be the teacher. Lord, release me from this prideful stronghold and help me trust You and others. In Jesus' name I pray, amen.

A fool is in love with his own opinion,
but wisdom means being teachable.
Proverbs 12:15 TPT

Fear Causes Wandering

Dear God, when I wander off from community, please bring me back into the fold. Let others notice my retreat and reach out. It's my deeply rooted insecurities that make me walk away. I become anxious that I'm not good enough or that I'm too much. I fear critical comments—the ones that rarely come. And rather than open up and share what I'm feeling, I fade into the background. Heal those wounds in me that continue getting triggered. Grow my desire and ability to trust friends and family. Please break this pattern in my life once and for all. I know this kind of change requires Your help. I can't do it without You. In Jesus' name I pray, amen.

Let the peace of Christ keep you in tune with each other, in step with each other. None of this going off and doing your own thing.
COLOSSIANS 3:15 MSG

Courage to Walk Out the Faith

Dear God, help me live a holy life that glorifies You. Let me be aware of Your presence every day, guiding my steps with intentionality. I want to be keenly aware of my words so I speak only truth. Let them be full of encouragement and hope for others to hear, advocating for You every time. Before I act, help me remember that someone may be watching every move I make. Let me be mindful as I walk out the day, letting my choices delight You. And above all, bless me with the courage to stand up for my faith even when I'm met with opposition. Make me bold to live and love for You. In Jesus' name I pray, amen.

*Let every detail in your lives—words,
actions, whatever—be done in the name
of the Master, Jesus, thanking God the
Father every step of the way.*

Colossians 3:17 msg

NUMBERED DAYS

Dear God, I don't want to waste a day worrying about things in my life. I don't want to be so overwhelmed with my own mess that I hide from community. Give me the wisdom to know when I need to focus on me and when I need to focus my time and effort on others, because sometimes I get it wrong. Before I was born, You determined my life. You decided the number of days I would be in the world. You set my path. Help me understand the purpose of my life, and bless me with the ability to walk it out with passion. Remove any fear that may keep me from being intentional in living for You. In Jesus' name I pray, amen.

Help us to remember that our days are numbered, and help us to interpret our lives correctly. Set your wisdom deeply in our hearts so that we may accept your correction.

PSALM 90:12 TPT

SUPERNATURAL INFUSION

Dear God, the Word is clear when it says my strength comes from You. It doesn't hint or mince words. It isn't vague, hoping I can decode the truth. No. The Bible straight up says my strength for the battles I face will be supernaturally imparted to me through our relationship. What a huge relief to know that I'll never be too weak. I have no reason to cower. With You, there is no reason to fear because I can't be defeated. As much as I try to figure everything out on my own, the truth remains that You are my source. Please build my confidence in You as I try to live out my life for You every day. In Jesus' name I pray, amen.

Now my beloved ones, I have saved these most important truths for last: Be supernaturally infused with strength through your life-union with the Lord Jesus. Stand victorious with the force of his explosive power flowing in and through you.

EPHESIANS 6:10 TPT

UNTOUCHED BY HUMAN LIMITATIONS

Dear God, this has been a long and difficult season of life. It feels like the world is working against me in every area. I'm struggling in relationships. My finances are a mess. I have very concerning health issues. My insecurities are screaming at me. And I have so much fear for the future. Please be big in my life right now. Give me courage to keep moving forward. Help me find confidence to advocate for my needs. And strengthen my heart to continue on, because I'm tired and weary and worried for so many things. What a privilege to serve a God untouched by human limitations. You're an unmatched resource for all good things, and I love You! In Jesus' name I pray, amen.

Don't you know? Haven't you heard? The LORD is the everlasting God, the creator of the ends of the earth. He doesn't grow tired or weary. His understanding is beyond human reach, giving power to the tired and reviving the exhausted.

ISAIAH 40:28–29 CEB

SCARED OF THE AGING PROCESS

Dear God, I'm terrified of the aging process. It feels very vain to tell You that, but I know I can tell You anything, and I'm grateful for that privilege. I worry that wrinkles and sags will make me less lovable—less attractive. What if I'm rejected? What if I feel irrelevant? It's just hard to watch my youth slip away. Remind me to cling to You when fear starts to rise. Give me perspective so I don't feel unwanted. Open my heart so I can embrace inevitable aging and find good things about it. Connect me with others who understand the changes we're facing. You are my Rock and are faithful to love me. Thank You! In Jesus' name I pray, amen.

When my skin sags and my bones get brittle,
GOD is rock-firm and faithful.

PSALM 73:26 MSG

Be a Climber

Dear God, I don't have to be afraid of anything because You have equipped me to walk out everything that comes at me. Be it a financial fallout or a ruptured relationship, I can stand tall as I follow Your lead through it. No health concern can scare me into giving up. No job loss can make me feel hopeless. As long as I take my worries right to You, my strength won't waver. When I choose to trust You, my faith will breed confidence and courage in my heart. You are the One who gives me what I need to continue on with a positive outlook. And together, we can climb every mountain. In Jesus' name I pray, amen.

The Eternal Lord is my strength! He has made my feet like the feet of a deer; He allows me to walk on high places.
<small>HABAKKUK 3:19 VOICE</small>

How to Stand in Victory

Dear God, it's hard to be paralyzed by fear when I'm busy living my life for You. I can't get trapped in anxiety when my energy is focused on doing Your will. When I'm passionate in my walk with You, I won't have time to worry about everything scary and difficult that I have to face. Thinking about Your goodness every day will keep me from being weighed down with the concern of my situations. I can see why loving You is the great commandment! Thank You for always making a way to stand in victory. Sometimes this dark world casts a shadow and I let it. When that happens, I'll know it's time to refocus my life on You. In Jesus' name I pray, amen.

"You are to love the Lord Yahweh, your God, with a passionate heart, from the depths of your soul, with your every thought, and with all your strength. This is the great and supreme commandment."

Mark 12:30 TPT

THE JOY OF THE LORD

Dear God, whenever I'm fearful of what's ahead, I will remember Your goodness in my life. When my sense of peace is being threatened as I walk through painful situations, I will delight in all the times You've been faithful to me. When I want to pull the covers over my head and give in to those pesky insecurities, I will instead joyfully praise You for who You are. Letting worry win is easy. It takes nothing for me to partner with panic. But if I am going to be a woman full of faith in a world that often feels dark, then I need to choose to let Your joy be what strengthens me. And I will. In Jesus' name I pray, amen.

He continued, "Go home and prepare a feast, holiday food and drink; and share it with those who don't have anything: This day is holy to God. Don't feel bad. The joy of GOD is your strength!"
NEHEMIAH 8:10 MSG

HE WILL MAKE
UP THE DIFFERENCE

Dear God, thank You for reminding me that I don't need to worry about having what's necessary for the battle ahead. My weakness actually opens the door for Your strength to flow through me. When I lack courage to soldier on because of fear or insecurity, I know You'll increase my confidence when I need it most. You'll motivate me to take the next step of faith as I walk through difficult times. I was never meant to do this alone! So rather than beat myself up for not being enough or wilting because I don't feel I have what it takes, I'll instead surrender to my weakness while I trust You to make up the difference. In Jesus' name I pray, amen.

But he answered me, "My grace is always more than enough for you, and my power finds its full expression through your weakness." So I will celebrate my weaknesses, for when I'm weak I sense more deeply the mighty power of Christ living in me.
2 CORINTHIANS 12:9 TPT

Let God Strengthen

Dear God, please make me strong. Make me wise. Bless me with keen discernment to know the path You have laid out for me. Give me confidence to navigate the hard seasons with bravery. Too often when I'm faced with the unknowns, I let fear take over. I worry about making the wrong choices, so I don't make any. I become paralyzed and ineffective by all the emotions swirling in my heart. Help me remember You aren't turned off by my struggles. I can't exhaust You. And when I am overwhelmed in life, scared of how things might turn out, I can trust that You will give me courage and peace to walk it all out. In Jesus' name I pray, amen.

God makes his people strong.
God gives his people peace.
Psalm 29:11 msg

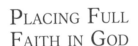

PLACING FULL FAITH IN GOD

Dear God, in those times when I feel attacked by my enemies, please see me. Let Your eyes be on me when I lack courage to advocate for myself. See my fear increase when I'm intimidated and scared. Be aware of every tear of sadness that streams down my cheeks. Know when I'm worrying and understand the details of my concern. See the confusion and chaos in my path. Help me navigate it all. Lord, I am counting on You to protect me. I am trusting that You will strengthen me for every difficulty. My faith is fully in You, believing You not only see me but also will give me what I need as I press on through life. In Jesus' name I pray, amen.

But the Lord is faithful and will give you strength and protect you from the evil one.

2 THESSALONIANS 3:3 CEB

Scripture Index